IGNITE YOUR CHAMPIONS

Build Your Business by Creating Connection and Community

TRACEY WARREN

Pacelli
PUBLISHING

Pacelli Publishing
Bellevue, Washington

Ignite Your Champions: Build Your Business by Creating Connection and Community

Published by Pacelli Publishing
9905 Lake Washington Blvd. NE, #D-103
Bellevue, Washington 98004
PacelliPublishing.com

Cover designed by Dawn Anderson, Tiny Stars Creative
Interior designed by Pacelli Publishing
Author photo by Dani McDonough Photography

ISBN-10: 1-933750-88-X
ISBN-13: 78-1-933750-88-0

Contents

Prologue

"Belonging is the opposite of loneliness. It's a feeling of home, of 'I can exhale here and be fully myself with no judgement or insecurity.' Belonging is about shared values and responsibility and the desire to participate in making your community better. It's about taking pride, showing up, and offering your unique gifts to others."
Radha Agrawal, *Belong*

I have thought of all sorts of ways to start this book.

More than anything, I want you to get through these first few pages and decide to keep reading.

While I hope you find the book brilliant, and finish it, my hope is that you continue to use it as a resource because of the impact the tools, tactics and ideas here can have on your life and business.

But more than that, I believe community has the power to change the world. Your community, mine, and all the others that can be created and cared for as a result of taking action on the words that follow.

Ultimately, I wrote it because I have watched and continue to watch so many people struggle with the simple things that could help propel their businesses forward--building relationships, creating community, and the impact those two things have on social media and content creation.

I can no longer watch the struggle knowing there is a better, and even easier way.

I promise to not "should" on you--or tell you what you "have to" do. There is no one right way to do any of this. This book is FULL of ideas--some you might love and some you might not. Take what you love and use it. Let the other ones go. No hurt feelings on my end.

Do you have any of this internal dialogue?

- I really don't like social media, but I know I need to use it.
- I don't know what to say.
- My ideal client is everyone. (Ugh)
- My customers aren't on social media.
- You must pay to play on any of the platforms.
- I don't want to annoy anyone.
- It all feels slimy.
- I don't want to sound like I'm selling used cars.

I hear these things all the time. I guess that makes them external dialogues as well.

If you have ever thought any of this about what you are trying to create, you are not alone!

We will likely be revisiting the internal discussions again as these thoughts might just be the beginning.

I would like to invite you to get curious, lean into what's possible and relax. Most of all, give yourself a TON of grace as you move forward. These tips and tactics take time, but you can put many of them into practice immediately. And when you do, you may start to see the benefits right away.

This is not a book you are just going to read through. Please use this book as a resource guide, a place to find ideas, explore something new and discover creative ways to find and nurture your own community.

There are blank sections throughout the book for you to answer questions. Write in it if youd like, or use your own notebook. But, doing the work and exercises will be key to your success.

This book is an invitation.

Thank you for responding with a yes.

Now, keep going.

I've got your back.

Food for Thought

What if you already knew everyone you needed to know to be ultimately successful in your business?

If you have been networking or in business for any length of time, this is likely the case.

Are there people who immediately come to mind when you think about your squad? Who are those who you know you can call anytime, or are there to support you when you ask for help, or even if you don't ask?

If you did already know everyone you need to know, imagine for a moment how that would or could change how you engage with the business world. I call these people champions and advocates. Later, you'll see ideas for discovering who these people are and how to develop them into raving fans. They may have already self-identified as advocates of yours without you doing anything. Take some action and they can become champions.

But first.

There are too many people trying to do "all the things."

Every new social media platform? They have an account.

Every networking event? They already RSVPd.

Someone requests a coffee date? They say yes.

TO ALL OF IT.

They do it because it may feel like part of the work they are "supposed" to do. Isn't that how to grow your business? It sure seems like that's how everyone else does it. Or is that just how you see it?

The problem is these are all busy activities that don't necessarily move the needle toward helping you grow your business. I recently heard a speaker ask, "Are you moving the needle or just polishing the dashboard?" Many of these activities fall into the latter.

In fact, it may start to look and feel like a "throw spaghetti at the wall and pray something sticks" approach.

But even more than that, it can start to LOOK like that to people who follow you online and off.

It's personally exhausting, frustrating and can leave you feeling like everyone else has this figured out, why don't you? It can also keep you stuck in mediocrity and broke. Ugh.

There really is a better way and that's what this book is about.

What I can tell you for sure is the tools, tips, tricks, and tactics in this book work, but it's about more than that. It's about a way of BEING, rather than what you are doing.

I have lived these principles for as long as I can remember and like the road less traveled, I have been identifying and igniting my champions along the way and it's made all the difference.

It can do the same for you.

Let's get clear about some of the words and phrases you will see throughout the book.

Initially, this book was going to be called *Nurture Your Network*. It was about nurturing the people in your life to build and create community--a concept I will define and a theme that will continue throughout this book.

Instead, this book is called *Ignite Your Champions* for a very specific reason. Nurturing is great, but many people can get stuck in a cycle of nurturing but never or rarely asking.

Igniting takes it a few steps beyond nurture. It helps others get fired up about what you are doing and gets them excited to share or even hire you for your expertise. There are also some great analogies around creating a spark and building a fire. Just you wait!

The Oxford dictionary defines *community* as 1) A group of people living in the same place of having a particular characteristic in common or 2) A feeling of fellowship with others, as a result of sharing common attitudes, interests, and goals.

As you continue through this book, you will see there is a lot about community creation that feels a little like magic. It's the feel-good stuff we crave at times. What you will also see is that it's so much more than that. There are tangible relational and financial results from building a business this way. (Some of those things are a little magical, too.)

We will be painting a picture of possibility. In doing so, I hope you can catch the vision for what makes igniting your champions important and the difference that can make for you and your business.

We will also be talking more about *champions and advocates* throughout this book and likely using those two terms interchangeably.

Champions are those people in your life and business you are choosing to connect with, spend more time with and make part of your ignition plan to continue to build that relationship.

Advocates are a result of the work you put in to nurture those relationships.

Let's change the way we look at social media--as an opportunity creator, rather than just a marketing tool--to build relationships and connect with the exact right people who will hire you, support you, or be a part of YOUR community.

Our journey is about to begin.

This is the road to creating community, to crafting client-attracting content and to doing it all with EASE!

I am beyond excited to be your guide.

This book will take you step-by-step through the FIRE framework in four key sections:

> **F** – Building a **Foundation**
>
> **I** – Starting the **Ignition**
>
> **R** – Building **Relationships** and Community
>
> **E** – Creating an **Engagemen**t and sales engine

Also, at the back of the book, we've gathered some resources to support you in continuing to stoke your own FIRE!

A little about myself--I have been a student of the hustle, so I know it well. For years when I ran my social media marketing company, I lived the definition of insanity, doing the same thing over and over and expecting different results.

It caused me to be WAY overextended with coffee meetings, networking events, and all those things that make us feel like we're "working." Yes, networking and coffee meetings can support your business, but not at the level I was doing them, because they caused me to not have time to do the work my clients hired me to do. To my family, it looked like I was working from the minute I got up until the minute I went to bed, often because that was the truth.

I also had profiles on all the social media platforms. That's what a good marketer does, isn't it?

This led to adrenal fatigue, exhaustion, staying stuck in mediocrity, and holding myself back from my potential.

When I realized this was what I was doing, I knew things had to change drastically.

What I saw in myself was the need for a more tightly-knit community I could build deeper relationships with, and a core group of people I could reach out to when I needed help instead of always trying to do things on my own.

I have grown to call these people my champions and advocates--people I intentionally nurture and stay in touch with on a regular basis. The results have been remarkable. It's amazing how people show up for you when you do the same for them.

In 2016, I was at an event, and we had to speak for five minutes about what we desire, with someone we didn't know. The other person wasn't allowed to say anything. And at the time, I was a social media manager, acting as an admin for multiple Facebook pages, which is part of why I felt like I was always working. What I said was, "I desire to not manage Facebook pages anymore and I desire to open a coworking space." And as soon as I said it out loud. I was like, "Oh crap. I didn't expect that to come out of my mouth."

In speaking those words, the idea of InSpark Coworking was born. The actual space opened 10 months later. The space is an in-person community of people in all sorts of roles--employees, business owners, etc.

But then, a friend suggested InSpark might just be a side hustle and this book and my new business is bringing me back to my social media roots.

That brings us to where I am today (and this book).

I recently read *Untamed* by Glennon Doyle, and a quote stuck out that felt like it was written for me. I share it here, because I believe the same can be true for you in your community creation.

> *"That night, a friend called and said, 'Glennon, here's what I've been thinking about all day: You made this community for other women. But maybe it was actually for you. All this time you've been creating the net you'd need to fall into.'"*

Cheers to building your own net.

Take Your Temperature

I invite you to take your social media temperature. This isn't saying that you must have all of these, but rather a check to see where you are right now, and as you progress through the book, you can use this information to inform decisions about how to proceed.

Knowing this will also help you make strategic choices going forward, which has the potential to save you time and money. Do you need to add or delete a platform? Focus on email marketing? This check can help you decide.

I also invite you to not overthink or judge yourself. This is a starting point.

If you get to a question and you have no idea how to answer, please move on. Everything in this section will be talked about later in the book, so if something isn't currently a part of your plan, it can be later if it's applicable! The best news--it might never be!

Consider what stories your online presence might be telling as well.

Before we talk about building your brand, you will want to see what your profiles are already saying about you. What do you want to be known for? Those key words, business roles and primary activities should be similar on each platform where you are active. There should be consistency. Whether your perfect client is checking you out on LinkedIn, Facebook, Instagram, or whatever platforms you have decided to make home, there should be a consistent message about who you are and what you do.

A confused mind won't buy.

And, as Brene Brown says in *Dare to Lead*, "Clear is kind. Unclear is unkind."

Let's go!

Do you have a blog? How often do you blog?

- Once a week
- Once a month
- Less than once a month, irregular pattern

Do you have an email newsletter?

- How many current subscribers do you have?

- Do you have a clear plan for getting people to join your email list, such as a lead magnet, community builder or other freebie?

- How often do you send an email to your list?

- What is your average open rate?

Do you have a Facebook business page?

- How many "likes" do you currently have?

- What is your reach? (Don't worry, you can make simple tweaks that can increase this number quickly – without paying any money.)

Are you active in Facebook groups?

- How many do you visit every week?
- Do you have your own group?
  - How many members?
  - Do you have a clear plan for growing your group?

Do you use LinkedIn?

- How many connections do you currently have?
- Do you post weekly?
- Do you use Instagram?
- How many people are you following?
- How many followers do you have?
- How often do you post?

What other social media platforms do you have/use?

- TikTok
- Clubhouse
- Twitter
- Other?

How often do you review your Google Analytics?

Have you done Facebook ads? Were they effective for you?

Do you have a business page on Yelp?

Do you have a Google My Business page?

What keywords do you use for SEO (Search Engine Optimization)?

What hashtags do you currently use for your business?

What are the other ways you communicate with potential clients?

- Postcards/mailings?
- Print ads?
- Group coupons?
- Phone calls?

How do you currently stay connected with current clients?

When was the last time you Googled yourself? (This can provide valuable information.)

Is your branding and language consistent across the platforms you choose to use?

Let's do a short content inventory:

- Do you have a podcast?
- Have you been a guest on podcasts? Do you keep a list with links?
- How many blog posts do you have?
- How many videos do you have?
- How many memes/graphics have you created?
- How do you capture your current content? Where do you save your graphics? How do you track ideas for potential content?

Mark a date on your calendar for three or six months out and look at this again. How have things shifted or changed for you?

What differences are you seeing because of the adjustments you've made?

Let's Go!
Do it your way instead of like everyone else. As you move on through this book, I will discuss several ways to achieve this.

If you have struggled with trying to be everyone else or feeling like you might sound like everyone else, stay tuned.

There is only one YOU. You don't have to be a megaphone for others and their message.

Be a megaphone for your own voice!

> *"You can't hire a secret."* – Michelle L. Evans

FOUNDATION

The Cricket Problem

"No business ever died from a shortage of attention. Companies and ideas fail because of a lack of resonance with the people they seek to serve."
Bernadette Jiwa, *Story Driven*

This is the complaint most often heard when it comes to social media. You take the time to write something thoughtful, make the words "just right" and you post it. Then, you wait.

And nothing. Crickets.

It can feel frustrating when this happens. It might also begin to feel like what you are doing is a waste of time.

It is not.

If this has been a challenge of yours as well, stay tuned.

There are solutions to get rid of those crickets for good and keep the conversation moving once you've gotten it started.

In the meantime, post and respond like someone's watching because chances are pretty good they are.

At times, social media can seem a bit lonely.

It can be a long, slow process that often feels pointless. It can seem like no one is even paying attention. Many people are what I call "lurkers." (I've also heard them called "listeners.") They see everything and rarely comment. But know they are there! And whether anyone ever comments, your efforts are not wasted, because search engines are always paying attention.

Want proof? For many of you, if you do a web search for your name, your social profiles will often show up on the first page. You can try that right now.

I'll wait.

Note here: if you have a name that is shared by many others, this may not work quite as well for you.

Hop Off the Hustle Hamster Wheel

I was chatting with someone recently and asking about their experience using Instagram Live, Reels and Stories and if they were getting the results they wanted. The answer was typical to what I have seen. "I'm just doing it; I don't have time to look at the results."

That's so sad to me. And it will keep them on the hamster wheel.

Results can help drive decisions for what stays and goes.

Stories are a way to share on each of the platforms that allow for live video, graphic sharing, etc. They also disappear after a set amount of time. And, since they go away, many feel compelled to keep creating and creating and creating. It's a never-ending cycle.

Multiply that across many platforms and you could be spending far too much time on social media--which may keep you feeling like you are doing "work." Unfortunately, it's work that is not moving the needle, but could keep you on the Hustle Hamster Wheel.

Without looking at your results, how do you know whether it's a good place to spend your time? You don't.

To be clear, results in this case are not about how many video views you got on one video or how many new people followed you. It's easy to get tied up in those numbers. One story usually won't have much impact for your business. Consistent stories may, but you must try it out for a while and then measure the effectiveness.

Hustle culture has taught us to just keep going, keep doing and somehow, we will reap the rewards. But that just isn't true. Hustle and grind culture has some other potential results in life and business.

It can:

- leave you exhausted. if you are always searching for the next big thing, whether a social media platform, new relationship, or business idea. It's exhausting, disheartening and can keep you in struggle.

- crush curiosity. Staying curious can support us in so many ways, but when you are exhausted, it's difficult to stay in that zone.

- lead to desperation. You may be doing all the things, but it isn't resulting in more revenue in your business. When that happens, it's easy to feel like you are just trying to stay above water. That can show up in all sorts of ways.

- make you feel you aren't enough. Everyone else is doing it this way, so I should too.

- keep you in business and financial mediocrity.

One Size Does NOT Fit All

There are all sorts of companies and/or, coaches who are selling cheap systems, templates, or blueprints for social media. You may have seen the ads for $27 this or $39 that. I have bought a couple myself as research for writing this book. What I have seen is content and a system that may work in the short term but isn't likely to provide a strategy for sustainable posting, engagement, and business growth.

If you do need support finding your voice, these can be helpful in the short term.

Also consider that if these "systems" are being sold by the thousands, then all that content just becomes part of the noise. It doesn't take long for your content to start looking and sounding the same as everyone else.

There really is no "one size fits all" plan for marketing.

Period.

As you progress through this book, it will become clear that it isn't about creating something new and brilliant every day or with every post. Doesn't that sound exhausting? I've tried to do it this way and I can tell you for sure that it is.

If you ever find yourself in an overthinking or overcomplicating loop, I've got you on that one too!

There is a better way.

Stick with me. We are going to get there.

The People Principle

Let's talk one more moment about the marketing people--coaches, consultants, "influencers" (pardon me, I just threw up in my mouth a little) who are hawking systems, templates, and "fill-in-the-blank" content calendars. They often talk about funnels, launches, lead magnets, and automations.

This is not a shaming or putting down of those tactics, but the important thing to remember is that your customers and prospects are ultimately people. These are humans you are attempting to engage with.

Businesses are often referred to as either B2B (Business to Business) or B2C (Business to Consumer) and while those designations may be true, it's only part of the story.

Business is about P2P--people doing business with other PEOPLE!

Let's think about it this way: *What if you looked at all of your marketing as relationship building?*

While ultimately, you want to grow your lists with lead magnets and other free content, there are humans on those lists. And because of that, you can assume or know a few things about them.

- They want to be seen and heard.
- They don't want to feel like a wallet.
- They want to solve their problems and are often willing to hire someone to help them.

- They want answers.
- They don't want to be slimed on.

What else do you assume about the humans you are trying to reach?

People don't want to be automated, blasted, or monetized.

Instead, they prefer connection.

Think of this as adding humanity to your marketing efforts.

- Be authentic. Your network WANTS you to be real! What does that look like?

- Ask for help.

- Ask for advice.

- Share who you are, not just what you do. Share your personality, sense of humor. (or not – don't try to manufacture humor if that isn't part of your nature) Share your humanness.

- Share the people behind your business. Behind the scenes content builds trust and curiosity. That is how people fall in love with your business!

More on all of this to come.

Keeping the human aspect in business and in your marketing will bring you more success with less efforts. It's about relationships, and if done strategically, can support you in creating a community that follows you wherever you go.

Know and Speak to Your Perfect Client

"People don't want to be lumped into a group categorized by age, marital status, and level of education. They want to be seen, understood and have their unique needs met based on their current reality. People want to be noticed as a unique individual."
Kelly Smith, *Willow and Oak Solutions*

This chapter isn't about finding your ideal customer and client. If you have been in business for any length of time, the hope is you've already done this work to understand who that person is.

You know who isn't your ideal client? Everyone.

Stick with me for a moment.

Yes, if you are a chiropractor, you can obviously work with "anyone with a spine." If you are sharing that on social media or at a networking group, though, the lack of specificity doesn't help those hearing it think of anybody. Though it might get a laugh from the group.

We each have a mental Rolodex of our connections. If you say "everyone," most can't specifically think of anyone.

Being specific allows others to think more clearly about the connections they have who might be a right or better fit.

If we revisit the chiropractor example, if they said instead, "We love to take care of people who've had a recent car accident or deal with chronic pain." That might allow those listening to think of someone specific.

Let's consider some other ways beyond the standard demographics to identify who these people are.

What is the mindset of my ideal person? Are they cautious or more of a risk taker? Do they want to know all the details, or do they make decisions more intuitively? Are they budget conscious, or do they easily see the value in pricing?

Knowing your ideal customer or client helps you know how to talk to them. You really can't talk to *everyone* on social media.

What other questions might you consider when you think about your potential clients and how you craft messaging that will pull the right people in?

Goals and Values

- What are the goals and values of your best customers?
- What are they trying to accomplish?
- What motivates them?
- What benefits do they want?

Problems and Needs

- What are their challenges?
- What keeps them up at night?
- What is getting in the way of their goals?
- What benefit are they looking for specifically?
- What will happen if they don't solve this problem or reach their goals?

Solutions

- What can you offer that will solve their problem?
- What results have your clients gotten before?
- How can you support them in reaching their goals?

Knowing these details can help you with your messaging so you attract exactly the right people and identify the platforms where you can best be discovered by them.

When you think about it, would you rather be boxed into an over 35, college educated, married woman with two children demographic, or seen as a mover and shaker who likes to be at the forefront of new ideas and technologies who is also willing to leap and follow their intuition?

If it applies to you, the latter might be more attractive.

Part of the challenge here might be that you think or have bought into the idea that you need a huge list or audience to be successful, but that just isn't true. Many entrepreneurs and coaches have built thriving businesses with lists of 500-1000 people.

This is the perfect place to introduce you to our first community leader.

Case Study: Sarah Duenweld, TheSwingShift.com

Co-Author of *Back to Business: Finding Your Confidence, Embracing Your Skills and Landing Your Dream Job After a Career Pause*

~~~~~

Bigger Isn't Always Better

Sometimes, collaboration for one thing can turn into everything.

That's what happened a few years ago when Sarah Duenweld and Nancy Jensen got together to solve a problem. Forty-six percent of women take a career break and many struggle to get back to work for various reasons. So they discussed "launching a program to get these women relevant (in the work force) again," Sarah said.

They developed a pilot program to see if there was a market for it, put the structure and curriculum together, got some speakers involved and found a corporate sponsor to add credibility and The Swing Shift was born. They got great feedback and their courses were selling out. And then people wanted more programs and services.

Their first priority was the education piece. "Let's get that out there and arm these women with the tools and resources they need to get a job, to make sure they can pivot to whatever they feel is empowering work to them," she shared.

The women took advantage of the educational piece and then came back because they wanted to support other women going through those same challenges. This worked perfectly because as this continued to grow, Sarah and Nancy couldn't always be available for questions. They needed the power of the community to help.

Some of these women just "needed to be reminded that their professional skills didn't go anywhere, if anything, they'd been enhanced." Sarah said.

They have added some structure for maximum benefit in their community of about 350 on Facebook. They created some smaller accountability groups that allowed for more sharing and greater vulnerability and deepening those relationships.

Their new clients come via word of mouth, through that community.

They are trying to come at all of this in a very authentic way. "That's how we've done everything. We've walked in their shoes before, so we know how they fit."

They have created the structure; they share what they know and have experienced, then they step out and meet with their groups on their own. "They are getting feedback amongst each other, are growing their network and they are helping," she said, "so they're not just getting help, but they're having the feeling of helping someone else because a lot of women don't have that in their lives right now, where they feel like they're contributing to someone else's life." Sounds like a magical win/win.

Build Your Basics

I am guessing that you already have some of your business basics mapped out--that information we have covered so far and have created it as you have started and grown your business. Finding the ideal customer was just the first part.

Let's talk about how you can create your own spark--since you can't start a fire without one--something that allows you to stand out from the noise of the crowd.

Here are a few key components that allow you to do this.

- Clear messaging
- Compelling why
- Mission, vision and purpose
- Core values
- Content buckets
- Knowing where to talk to YOUR people. (AKA platforms)

Let's take a deeper look at each of these individually.

Clear Messaging

I am not a messaging expert and would never claim to be. What I am is a witness. I pay attention to words and know when it's off. It can be the simple difference between someone introducing themselves as a mortgage broker (yawn) or a mortgage matchmaker. Which one makes you lean in to learn more? And yes, both are accurate, but if you sound like everyone else, it's easy for whoever is listening to tune out the ordinary.

There have been people on my friend lists who have pivoted their businesses so fast and hard, it made my head spin. So, what are they? A business coach? A time management expert? A book writing consultant? Looking at their posts, it's not clear.

If your messaging isn't clear, what happens?

- You may stay in struggle. If you can't clearly share about what you do, others won't be able to either. That means it may be challenging to refer you. That could lead to struggling to launch in a profitable and sustainable way.

- You may get BAD referrals. This is a great gauge to let you know.

- Your marketing will be challenging and less effective. Being clear helps you create and determine what content is "right" for you.

- You aren't making an obvious, well marked path for your ideal client to come to you.

- You aren't building the know, like and trust factor.

Mediocre messages lead to mediocre results.

You can't out-hustle confusing content. If your messaging isn't clear, no amount of repetition is going to help.

Clear messaging makes it easy for the right people to find you and hire you because they already know you are the exact fit for them!

If you want to make your message a movement, it MUST be clear, concise, and easy to repeat! This is one way to stand out in a crowded marketplace.

Think about it. Can other people share about your business in a succinct way? If not, there might be some shifts to consider moving forward.

Resource alert! Check out Dr. Michelle Mazur's book, 3 *Word Rebellion* if you want some DIY messaging support. It is worth mentioning here that working with Michelle is what brought me to my own 3 Word Rebellion, *Ignite Your Champions*.

Compelling Why

If you aren't familiar with Simon Sinek and his TED Talk about *Start with Why*, I highly recommend you watch his take on the idea. A great why can get people ON your bandwagon. It has the potential to get people fired up to want to know more about you and what you do.

Your WHY acts as a compass. It provides a path for your journey, can help with making choices and be an invitation for others to join you.

My why is about supporting women in business, because I know when women make more money, we have the power to influence change in the world. More specifically, I want revenues of $500K per year, so that I can invest $50k per year in women-owned businesses that might normally get overlooked by typical investors.

There are more specific steps and goals around that, but the deeper you can *feel* your why, the easier it will be to allow it to motivate you when things get tough.

Mission, Vision, Purpose

"Seemingly powerless people, fueled by their deepest--even sometimes un-nameable--sense of meaning find those who share a cause or purpose and act together, without needing to be told what to do, to make a dent."
Nilofer Merchant, *The Power of Onlyness*

This is not a section about how to create your mission and vision statement, or about defining your purpose. There are lots of tools out there for helping you do that.

What I want you to understand is how important it is to express those in your marketing. When you share about your mission, it brings other people along. When you talk about your vision, it helps other people see and dream bigger for you and sometimes for themselves. When you speak your purpose, it can help support your audience in knowing who else might make a great introduction for you.

Dreams are part of the MVP (mission, vision, purpose) and can inspire, motivate, and give permission for those around you to see that bigger things are possible.

Share your visions and dreams. This is another way to get people excited about the work you do.

How clear is your MVP? Can people repeat it to others? If they can, that's how your community can grow beyond your immediate connections. It makes it so easy to introduce you, in real life or virtually. It helps others identify who a perfect introduction is!

What is the brilliance you want to be known for?

And, just like all other marketing, this isn't something you can share once and move on. It needs to be stated over and over.

Core Values

How do your core values show up in your business?

Again, if you aren't clear on what your core values are, a quick internet search for "core values exercise" will deliver several quick options.

What words or themes are most important to you? For me, it's about connection, community, fun and freedom. Knowing this helps inform decisions in my business beyond content creation.

Knowing your core values can support you in creating your messaging, identifying content buckets, creating curiosity, and attracting the right clients to your business, so they are important to know and share.

Content Buckets

We are going to talk more about content buckets later in the book, but where your content can go wrong is when you are talking about too many things. It confuses potential buyers if they must keep guessing what you do. If you had to dial down what you really LOVE to talk about, what would those three topics be?

Again, more on this later. This is food for thought.

If you have initial ideas, take a moment to jot them down.

What topics might be in your content buckets? What are the first few things that come to mind?

Platforms

This will not be a discussion about what to post on each platform. They change too often to include that here, but each one offers distinct benefits--even as much as they are all trying to be like each other. (Darn it anyway.)

There is only so much time in a day and getting involved on every platform isn't realistic or warranted. You need to know where your current customers and prospects are before you begin. It's so easy to see something new as a bright shiny object that "could" bring you success. Pause, take a deep breathe, evaluate and then decide.

It can be tempting to feel like you need to be on every social media site, and maybe over time, you can invest in using a number of sites, but start small. Figure out where your prospects and their connections are hanging out and start there. Having a profile on LinkedIn and a business page on Facebook are good starting points. Or, if you prefer Instagram to Facebook, that's also a great place to begin.

Pick a platform, love it hard.

This is important because it can take time to gain some momentum and traction. I have heard people say, "Well, I tried it for a couple weeks and it just didn't work." Of course, it didn't. That isn't nearly enough time to even begin to make a dent.

Commit for three or even six months. Be consistent—however that looks for you and then evaluate. However, as you will see as you continue this journey, it's valuable to be testing, measuring, and shifting throughout the process.

Social Media Simplified

It would be remiss for us to start discussing social media without clarifying a few things first.

Social is about opportunity and being open to what that might look like for you and your business. It is not an absolute and is certainly not the end-all, be-all for marketing your business. It could mean potential new business partnerships, collaborations, and introductions. And it absolutely helps build increased visibility, brand recognition and your online reputation.

It's important to know why you are there, and how your presence fits into the rest of the marketing you are doing. What are you trying to accomplish?

It's not about sales, or ROI (Return on Investment), although both can be considered results. What if you looked instead at ROR (Return on Relationship)?

What's the ROI of social media? If I never had to answer this question again, I would be one very happy woman. As was just mentioned, social media is part of an overall marketing and community creation plan, so it can be especially challenging to put a dollar value on it.

What you will see, though, as you continue to read, are real life stories of the power and financial benefits of growing your business this way--and social media can play an integral role in that.

Consistent social media allows you to stay top of mind as well.

When you post content on a regular basis, it's like a virtual tap on someone's shoulder, or drip--but the best kind of drip. You share great information, add value, offer yourself as a resource and when someone needs what you have to offer, they will remember (or you are giving them a better opportunity to remember) the value you have given along the way. Partner this social media strategy with a champions and advocates touchpoint plan and WOW!

Quick reminder: social media is a marathon, not a sprint. You don't plant a seed and then yell at it to grow. Treat social media marketing and igniting your champions the same way, planting a seed, watering, and nourishing it and you can cultivate the rewards and relationships over time.

There are many things social media is about and many things it is not about. It might be easier to start with what it is NOT.

- It is not a place to blast your marketing message as loud and as often as possible. Be aware that if you have a business page and a personal page on Facebook, you shouldn't be posting the same content on both. Also know that if you are a member of local groups and post your content on those, everyone who is your friend will see those posts over and over in their newsfeed. If it looks like spam to the reader, it will repel, rather than attract your ideal client.

- It is not a replacement for all other marketing methods. It is a part of the marketing pie. And while you may see some success from just sitting behind a computer and plugging away, you will have more success when you mix your online and offline activities to promote your business.

- It is not a popularity contest. In fact, studies have shown that the bigger your audience/followers number grows, the harder it is to get people engaged in the conversation.

- It is not a place to market without a strategy. Developing and creating a content strategy and identifying who EXACTLY you would like to be reaching will give you greater success.

Now, let's talk about what it is:

- It is a great place to connect and to share--ideas, items of value, etc. It is important to note here that when I say connect, I don't mean inviting everyone you have ever met to become your Facebook friend. In fact, that tactic can get you put in Facebook jail (the term used to describe what happens when FB limits your ability to use their site). There are a number of things you can do to get there--another benefit to reading the Terms of Service. True connection is about giving, not taking. The more socially savvy people get, the easier they can spot a salesperson trolling their newsfeed and friend requests.

- It is a great addition to most marketing strategies. In my years on social media, there have been only a few people whose businesses wouldn't benefit from using social media and don't really "fit." If you have picked up this book, I'm guessing that isn't you.

- It is a great place to grow your business when done correctly.

- It is the perfect place to collaborate, build others up, share ideas and support each other's businesses.

- It is a powerful marketing tool. In fact, for many savvy computer and social media consumers, you aren't a legitimate business unless you have a social media business page.

- It is a place to build and share your expertise. The knowledge you have gathered in working your business or gaining your education allows you to answer questions and address your topic online. That builds the know, like, trust factor and makes it easier for those in your audience to narrow down their search when they are looking for someone in your line of work.

Bonus tip: Keep the platform ON the platform.

In the spirit of being everywhere all the time, many have "simplified" this by sharing the same exact content on all their platforms.

That is a rookie mistake--unless it's intentional. Some know this may not be as effective, but they don't care. You get to choose.

Each platform has very distinct ways to communicate and measure success, from video to hashtags and even the language they use. When someone is sharing from one platform to another, it can be confusing to your audience on the platform where it is shared.

Different platforms truly do have different "languages." Symbols like # and @ are perfectly appropriate and useful on some sites and not on others.

Some platforms prefer everyday language. And, while these are general rules, you can test with your own audience to see what's most effective.

I've heard it shared like this, "If I wanted to see your TikToks, I would be there, but I'm not, so I don't." Because of this, sharing exactly the same thing everywhere can be repelling.

This book is about sharing how to build your business by creating community, and this practice does not forward that goal.

What is the Right Platform?

There are some who say that a business owner should be on every platform. Just do it. That is not what you will hear here. It's just not a practice that is realistic or sustainable for most business owners who are a company of one.

There are social media channels for everyone, so taking a little time to find the best one(s) for you is time well spent.

The biggest challenge with this spray and pray (putting your marketing and messaging everywhere and praying it's effective) approach to your social media marketing and community creation is it's destined to leave you stretched too thin, exhausted, and completely ineffective. (See Hustle Hamster Wheel) It's the equivalent of doing the same thing over and over and expecting different results--isn't that called insanity?

The other downside is it can make you feel like you are doing marketing activities and checking them off your to-do list, but could also have you wondering why it isn't working.

When choosing platforms that are best for you, consider the following:

Who is using which platform? This information can ebb and flow, but it's also very easy to find with a quick search. For most people, LinkedIn is an absolute yes and then their second choice is often Instagram or Facebook. If you aren't sure, these are great places to start.

It's also important to note that every platform seems to be in a race to be like the other ones. (I wish they would stay in their own lane.) It started out that "stories" were only on one platform, and now they are everywhere. The same is true for the evolution from the like button to "reactions."

This isn't always about where your ideal client is. It's about where their connections are spending time, too. I hear people say all the time that their ideal clients are not on Facebook. While that may be the case, it's also where the most people ARE hanging out and chances are your people ARE connected to the people who spend time on Facebook.

Where do YOU like spending time? If you don't like a specific platform or feature on the platform, don't feel compelled to use it. Personally, I don't enjoy stories. They can take a lot more time. (I know they can also be very effective.) They just aren't for me.

When it comes to stories and reels and other features of each channel, consider doing them based on what you want to do AND what your audience wants.

I'm assuming you got into business to spend time doing what you love, not hanging out on social media all day!

Note: Be aware of the latest and greatest!

Several years ago, there was a video platform called Periscope. Many business owners, including myself, went all in on Periscope--recording videos regularly, trying to grow my following, etc. But, within a short amount of time, it started to lose steam, and then became irrelevant altogether.

At that time, going "live" became an option on Facebook. So, for many, that meant that instead of building an audience on a new platform, we could spend time engaging, through live video, on a platform we had already been building for years.

There will always be someone trying to "do it better" than Facebook. But for many, many people, they have invested a lot of time making connections there.

Building up an audience on any new platform can take a lot of time. Be strategic and intentional when considering adding anything new.

IGNITION

Build Know, Like and Trust

I'm assuming you've heard before that people do business with those they know, like and trust.

We have talked briefly about opportunity, and building the know, like and trust factor is one way we can be creating opportunities.

When you post online, you can either be building trust or tearing it down. For a business owner to be most effective, focusing on what builds trust will be the biggest help. This is applicable on your business and personal profiles.

Things that build:

- Using language for the platform on the platform. When you share one piece of content and have it shared everywhere, it can break down trust.

- Being human. Ultimately, we are all in the people business. Using language that is more natural is attractive!

- Sharing authenticity and vulnerability. The innerwebs are getting rather tired of what I call "cotton candy content." More about this momentarily.

- Clear messaging.

- Making it easy for people to find and reach out to you. Your contact information should be in all the obvious places, so when someone is ready, they can easily contact you.

Things that destroy:

- Not checking facts before posting. There are several celebrities who have died multiple deaths because of misinformation getting shared.

- Sharing "copy and paste" posts. Totally useless for building your brand and expertise. (Yes, even on your personal profile.)

- This one is usually relevant to the ladies, but your profile should look like you do in real life.

- Don't tag 99 friends to get more "visibility."

- Violating the terms of service. Most users of these platforms have made a habit out of clicking the box that says they agree to the terms of service, without ever reading them. Take a few minutes to read them now. The profile you save may be your own.

Authenticity, Vulnerability and Verbal Vomit

"We've gone too far into manufactured friendship through social media and something different is coming next. The pendulum is swinging back to genuine, authentic human connections."
David Meerman and Reiko Scott, *Fanocracy*

We talked about how people do business with people. And that is definitely true. But as I said, they are getting tired of the cotton candy stuff--the "everything in my life is perfect" BS that also seems to fill our social media feeds.

You have friends like this don't you? Their relationships are perfect, their children are straight-A students and their life and business are thriving. Did you also know there are actual companies out there that do "lifestyle branding" photos with cars, boats, real estate, etc. so you can show a "dream" on your feed that is a total fake?

We're onto you, fake people!

People crave relationship and connection. You get that through face-to-face interactions AND you can also get that by showing who you really are.

If I just scared you a little, please stick with me on this.

There is a huge difference between being authentic and vulnerable and verbally vomiting all over your social media followers.

Authenticity helps allow people to get to know you. It can show up whenever you do and over time, your audience will feel like they do know you. When you get on a call, there is already trust built up.

Or think of it this way--you go to a networking event, and you meet someone. They may need to hire you now, or not. But they will find your social media channels, and they will watch your work. Are you who you say you are? Do you already have advocates for your brand? When you stay top of mind, those potentials customers will call you when they have a need.

The reverse is also true if they discover you online first and watch and listen to what you say. If they then meet you in person and who you are in real life doesn't match, that's trouble.

Verbal vomit is what happens when people take their realness a little too far. Social is not a digital diary. It is also not necessarily a place to process when you are in the middle of a huge mess.

Also, consider your industry and how you share. If you are a financial advisor/planner, you may not want to share about being broke. If you are in healthcare, please don't talk about bad choices you are making where your health is concerned.

One other note: You don't have to have an opinion about everything--or maybe more accurately you don't have to share your opinion about everything on social media.

Also, you don't have to give everyone else's opinion your ear. (Block, snooze, and unfollow can be your friends!) Boundaries, baby!

Take imperfect action.

Be willing to show the messy parts of your life.

Done is better than perfect.

Take baby steps if you need to but do it.

Create Curiosity with Content

"If you're going to take the time to put out content, let's make sure it's relevant to your desired outcome. Otherwise, it's just noise--and you don't want to contribute to just noise. That won't attract people to you."
Nikki Rausch, *Sales Maven*

When creating content, there is a range between completely useless to thought-provoking and engaging and a whole lot of stepping stones along the way. I call this the Curiosity Curve.

Your content increases in effectiveness and reach on a continuum.

On one end of the spectrum, you have posts that are vague, random, copy and paste junk, and sheep posts (trends that everyone seems to jump on that do nothing to help you and your brand stand out.)

Then you have another group of posts that are equally annoying and also not helpful--overselling, slimy tactics (PM or DM me for details) or sharing things that aren't fact-checked.

But, on the positive side, you can quickly build not just curiosity, but interest, value and thought leadership by:

- Adding value--Sharing about those things you know that will benefit your audience

- Being a resource for your audience

- Sharing items in your content buckets (We will dig into this in a bit.)

- Asking questions

- Sharing stories

- Clear messaging (yes, this is an ongoing theme)

Over time, doing these things will give you credibility, thought leadership, influence and help you become an industry of one, rather than just another voice that adds to the noise.

Another facet to creating curiosity is what it does for your audience. When you share online or off, are people leaning in or commenting to find out more or does the conversation end after what you have shared?

Let me share two social media examples:

a. At XYZ Real Estate, we help our clients find the house of their dreams. If you are looking for something right now or know someone else who is, we would love to help. Please give us a call.

b. So excited that we just helped a family of five find the perfect house. The girls in the family are most excited about having three bathrooms! How many bathrooms are in your ideal home?

Which one makes you most interested in learning more?

A key to community-creating content is about inspiring curiosity. Business owners tend to be on a spectrum between not sharing often enough about how people can hire them and what they can hire them for, and too frequently sharing the same thing. It's about finding a mix. Some say asking people to do business 10 to 20 percent of the time is about right. I say that content creation is a constant process of measuring, refining and testing again.

Don't Let Social Media Dominate Your Life

Social media doesn't need to dominate your life. Here are a few ways to simplify your content creation.

As a business owner, your cup is likely always running over with a never-ending list of things that must get done.

An editorial calendar can help you drain one item from the cup.

Are you familiar with the story of the jar and the rocks? A teacher put a jar in front of his class and filled the jar with large rocks and then asked them if it was full. They said yes and then the teacher added smaller rocks that fit into the nooks and crannies and asked the same question again. He then added smaller pebbles, and next added sand.

The gist is you need to put big rocks (or your biggest priorities) into the jar first.

You can do the same with your content calendar.

Get a blank calendar for each month and start adding the important dates and events that are happening soon.

If you plan like this, it gives you a starting point for what to post, and when.

Take a moment to think about the magazines you might see at the grocery store checkout--*Vogue, Cosmopolitan*, etc. If you lined up magazines for every February for the last few years, what do you think you might see?

Valentine's ideas, fashion for Spring, some quiz about finding the love of your life.

They don't reinvent the wheel every year. There are themes that run throughout, and my guess is your business is the same.

Consider this as you are planning content for yourself.

- What are the recurring things that happen in your business?
- Are there events that happen regularly?
- Are there seasons where sales are up or down?
- What are the trends that happen every year?
- How does your business line up with school calendars?

I hope you get the idea.

You can take that information and plan for your upcoming three, six or even 12 months based on those trends.

Batch your content creation. Batching your content creation is a great way to maximize your creative brain AND save time.

Sitting down at your computer and thinking about what to post on a daily or weekly basis can be exhausting and isn't a sustainable way to do your marketing activities.

Take 30 minutes to plan and/or schedule your content for the week. When you do this, you may find it increases ideas and creativity, which allows content to flow more freely.

Keep a running list of ideas for times when you might not be feeling as creative. I personally use Airtable (an online tool like Excel, but with much more capability--and it's prettier) for capturing these ideas when they are flowing, but you can use whatever tool works best for you.

Create daily, weekly or monthly themes. Break down your content creation even further (if it serves you) by creating themes for each month, week, or even day.

In the reference section of this book, I have listed monthly and daily holidays and observances that could be helpful as you consider this.

How do these theme days make content creation easier? If you know that for the month of May, you are going to be talking about _____, it's easy to know if a piece of content fits or doesn't. In addition, if you know every Tuesday, you are going to share a tip of some kind, it's really easy to gather a number of tips and schedule those out over a few weeks at a time.

Alliterative theme days. (I love alliteration!) Use hashtags for these on LinkedIn and Instagram, or based on your audience. Keep in mind what makes sense for you and your business. If you are a financial planner, you might want to avoid something like Wild Wednesday, but Word Wednesday could be a perfect option for you to share industry jargon that many don't understand, but also won't necessarily ask.

You may already know this but when you use these as hashtags, be sure to not use spaces between the words.

Make it happen Monday

Mantra Monday

Money Monday

Make an impact Monday

Motivation Monday

Talk it up Tuesday

Testimonial Tuesday

Tip Tuesday

Wild Wednesday

Wisdom Wednesday

Wild Wednesday

Word Wednesday

Thankful Thursday

Thoughtful Thursday

Think about it Thursday

Throwback Thursday

Fun Friday

Feelings Friday

Freedom Friday

Five Star Friday--a creative way to share your great reviews

Flashback Friday

Safety Saturday

Selfie Saturday

Self-Care Saturday

Posting tools are another way to simplify.

There are so many tools out there to make content and community creation simpler. The key is to find tools that work for you. You may ask others in your community what they use, but there are so many options. Take advantage of free trials if that gives you the chance to test and see what might work for you.

Also, beware of the small subscriptions. It's so easy to sign up for several tools that cost between $5 and $20 per month, and before you know it there is way too much money going out the door without good justification.

Templates are my last simplification tip for this section. When it comes to creating graphics, one way to make it easier is creating templates. You can create 10 to 12 that are branded and have your web address on them, then simply change out the words. Viola! Templates make creating memes and visuals so simple!

For example, if you know you want to take advantage of #FiveStarFriday, you could create one graphic to use over and over but change the words based on the testimonial.

Let's Talk about Content

"You don't become unstoppable by following the crowd.
You get there by doing something better than anyone else can do it."
Tim Grover, *Relentless*

I want to take a few moments to talk to anyone in any business where it feels like the market is saturated.

The worst thing you can do when building your business and trying to create a community and all the goodness that can bring is to sound like everyone else. That can leave you drowning in the Sea of Sameness.

Real estate is a great example of this. Most agents post the same exact kind of content--open houses, and successful sales. That is great information, but you might add something unique to help you stand out.

Here is a good litmus test: When you are writing or talking about your company or product, could you easily replace your company name with any other company in the same industry?

- If the answer is yes, you may need to switch it up to create visibility for you and your brand.

- If the answer is no, congratulations! You are on the right track.

Ask yourself a few questions:

What if your content acted as an invitation? How can you use your content to invite them into a discussion? This might take a little creativity, but it's also another way to show the human side of your business.

How can you build curiosity into your content creation? It's not always about telling them exactly what to do and how they can hire you. Sometimes, it's the subtle stories you tell that leave them wanting to hear more from you.

What are some example stories that immediately come to mind that you can share that shine the light on the unique work you do in the world?

Use **keywords** in your content, but in a human way. Know your keywords and use them! How do people search for you? That is helpful information to help you know which words to use. You may think it's "forgiveness," but what people are searching for is, "How to not hate my spouse." (hahaha)

It's easy to get so caught up in your business that you think you know exactly what they (your prospects) might be looking for, but when you open your mind to new ideas, you might be surprised what is actually in their search bar.

If you still are wondering what you might share, keep going!

What Are You Going to Talk About?

If you are getting stuck around your own content creation, (it happens to the best of us!) use these questions as prompts to help you discover where you can start more conversations or be a resource to your online communities.

In the following section, there will be tons of other suggestions for your content creation. These questions can get your brain flowing.

What questions do people always ask you about your product or service?

What do you find you are always educating people about?

What myths about hiring someone like you can you debunk?

How will someone save time or money by hiring someone like you?

What kind of checklists, templates, or infographics could you create to support your clients?

What excites you most about the work you do?

Who are experts in your industry you have learned from?

What are the common misconceptions about your industry?

What industry terms can you simplify?

What is the weirdest response you've gotten about the work you do?

Share some customer success stories.

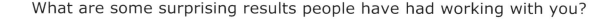

What are some surprising results people have had working with you?

What industry specific books would you recommend to your audience?

What Are Your Content Buckets?

Often, people talk about way too many things on social media. When they do, it makes it challenging for others to talk about them. I want to make it as easy as possible for people to say, "If you need to hire someone for _____, this is the exact person you need to know for that."

When it comes to curiosity, you can be clever, but it's more important to be clear. Some people can clever their way into causing confusion and that tends to drive people away rather than pull them closer. You want your audience of followers to lean in to hear or desire to learn more.

I encourage everyone to have between five and six content buckets. One bucket must be offers and promotions (because you do have to ask for business from time to time). A couple other buckets could be client stories (great for creating curiosity), events, and sharing about members (if that is applicable).

The other three buckets should be topic/expertise related.

When you have designated content buckets you can use them as a filter for all your content. For example, with my coworking space, our three topics are productivity, creativity, and community. All content that isn't about promotions, members, and events goes through this filter. So, when looking at a leadership quote, I don't post that because it isn't the three topics I mentioned.

Ask yourself some questions to help you get started with ideas.

What do you want to be known for?

What are you an expert at?

What do you do better than anyone?

Let's do a content bucket brainstorm. Yay, another exercise!

First, start a timer for five minutes. Write down everything you could possibly talk about relating to your business and expertise. GO!

You may have categories and sub-categories as part of this list.

Now, it's time to whittle down these ideas.

Are there topics on this list that could be combined?

If you dial this down and combine the topics, that can give you your content buckets.

Do you have two or three topics you can use to help create your content? Add that to the other "required" buckets and you should have five or six to use going forward.

Congratulations!

Content Buckets

Sales/Offers

Content Ideas (Tons of Them)

"Different is better than better." – Sally Hogshead

You could literally fill your entire year with these ideas I'm about to share partnered with your expertise.

So many ask the question about how often and when to post and my response is always test, measure, adjust and test again. I am finding less content is better now more than ever. Less, but better. More authentic.

Be sure to talk with, not at. Just pushing content rather than starting and inviting a conversation can be off-putting. If your content is all about you, it may not be having the effect you would like. Make it about your audience and they will be more likely to engage.

Share your story. Remember at the beginning of this book, I talked about sharing your why, mission, vision and purpose? Those are all important stories for you to tell, not just once, but often.

Do you have a new goal you are working toward? What are you excited about in your business right now?

People connect with and remember stories, so finding a way to collect and share these in different ways will serve you well.

Did you know? This is a great way to post statistics and other information. Instead of sharing as a statement, turning it into a question invites more conversation. Sample ideas: "Did you know that when the stock market drops, interest rates on home loans tend to do the same?" or "Did you know that for small businesses, we offer QuickBooks setup and training for those who aren't quite ready to hire a bookkeeper?

What are some "did you know" questions you can ask?

Ask questions. So often, when people say they aren't getting engagement, it's because they aren't asking for it.

The questions should be something they can answer with just a few words.

Amy Porterfield, host of *Marketing Made Easy* podcast says, "If you post, 'Tell us your favorite story about your mom,' most people might think about it for a few seconds and then decide they don't want to take the time to answer or respond. Instead, post, 'What is one word you would use to describe your mom?' That makes it super simple for people to answer."

Make it easy for people to engage!

What are some of the questions you get asked all the time? Address those with text, blogs or video. These are perfect for creating content! What are the regular questions people ask about your product or service?

If you write blog posts or create videos for each one, that makes it easy to share the next time someone poses the same question.

Consider also what people don't know about the work you do. What are the questions they aren't asking but need to know about? Many of your prospects don't know what they don't know. Sharing that information with them ahead of time will be helpful!

Do you already have some questions that come to mind?

What are the questions people might ask you about the work you do? Social media is a perfect place to tell them BEFORE they even ask.

Share about someone in your network. Who are the other people you know and admire in your network? This is a great way to shine the light on others in your community, but also shows that you are the person who knows people.

How does that benefit you? People will come to you for recommendations! In addition, it creates curiosity about YOU! That's a serious win/win!

Remember this strategy when you start talking about champions and advocates, because sharing about THEM is a great way to ignite!

Tell customer success stories. The key to this kind of share is to make it as succinct as possible when you can. If you are a coach, that could look like this, "Working with a new client today and based on our phone call, she turned around and had this specific success." The story doesn't have to be long to have impact.

What are the results clients experience from working with you? Tell your audience about them.

Bonus: If you can share success stories based around the different ways you work with people.

- In a client strategy session today, this was a breakthrough.
- In a group Zoom call today, this cool thing happened.
- During a networking event today, this was a simple tip that really resonated.

Definitions of words. Choose a word of the week. Many businesses have very specific industry words. Often, we assume that everyone knows what all those words mean, such as fiduciary, amortization, revenue, APR, due diligence, rendering, vector, SEO, etc. I could go on and on based on YOUR industry, but I hope this provides you a starting point.

There are likely many words you know, use, and completely understand because they are part of your everyday conversation.

What are some of the words you use on a regular basis that may cause confusion for your audience?

Share your online reviews. To make this easy, create a graphic template in Canva or PicMonkey (or your preferred tool) and change out the words. As a bonus, ask people if you can share their full name and business. Since most of those online reviews already have their full name attached, their answer will most certainly be yes. This lends more credibility to the review.

Of course, if your industry has rules and regulations around this, proceed accordingly.

Be sure to include reviews from a wide variety of people (especially in different ideal client profiles) and check ALL places they can leave a review! Also share the "hidden" reviews! On Yelp, they only have a certain number of reviews that are visible, so dig into the hidden ones to find review gold!

Testimonials. Capture video testimonials from people you have worked with, especially when they represent your ideal client. If you host live events, set up a place at the location to record these moments right after. If video testimonials aren't possible, you can copy and paste testimonials and recommendations from all the locations they are posted like Yelp, Google and social platforms.

Photos. Great images are a way to create curiosity and potentially stop the scroll. It can help get you out of the "sea of sameness" or the wall of words that typically fill up a feed. How can you make your photos stand out? People can be a huge part of this, but also try some different things to change it up. Make an image black and white or capture parts of your life and business that most people don't typically get to see.

If you are launching a new business, "behind the scenes" or "how things are progressing" images can create excitement and get people on board even before you open!

It will serve you well to develop a habit around taking photos in and around your business. You just never know what you might capture in the background that will get and keep a conversation going online.

Share interesting facts and statistics about your industry. This is a really simple way to develop and share your expertise. It's also a great way to highlight your personal style--bringing humor into it if that is part of who you are.

Articles on YOUR expertise. Not every piece of content you share needs to be created by you. Share industry articles around your topic. To make them most effective, add your comment on the article you are sharing. If it's an article about 10 Productivity Hacks, you might post, "Here's a great list of productivity hacks. What might you try right away?"

Side notes about this: Facebook doesn't particularly love outside links that take you off Facebook, so they can be most effective on LinkedIn. Test it for your audience and see how they respond. For every rule, there always seem to be exceptions.

If your industry is in the news, this is another opportunity to be a part of the conversation.

Videos. First of all, they should look compelling to play.

You do yourself a huge disservice by titling a video with something vague like, "Here is what's new." A great title that tells someone exactly what they will get by watching will be the difference between people stopping to watch or scrolling right by.

Good sound and lighting are also important but are not paramount. There are times for professional video and other times where your phone is a perfect recording device.

This is the online representation of you. Make it count, but don't get caught up in making it perfect, either. Authenticity is more important than perfection.

This is another area where you can try, test, measure and adjust. How long should your video be? Let your audience tell you in the metrics you see.

Motivational or other quotes. I share this idea with a few caveats.

- If your posts look like everyone else's, they won't get noticed. So just putting a quote on a pretty graphic may or may not do anything for your business.

- Make sure it has your branding or website on it.

- Give credit where credit is due. If you know the source of the quote, please attribute accordingly. (This is a place where it's good to do your due diligence to make sure you are giving proper attribution.)

- Make sure the quote falls into one of your content buckets.

Share about each of your products or services. In the spirit of being of service, this can easily get glossed over. Yes, we are here to build relationships and create community. We are also here to SELL!

- What are the features and benefits of each? If you don't know the difference between these two, take a moment to familiarize yourself. Many people focus too much on the features (the what), instead of the results of what your product or service will provide.

- Who are they best for? The more specific you can be about this question, the easier it is for the exact right people to opt in!

- What can someone expect from each?

Promotions. This may sound self-explanatory, but this is one of the biggest ways people miss the mark on social media. Remember, we often feel like we are sharing SO MUCH about our businesses, but with the algorithms and how people use the platforms, we have to be WAY more repetitive than we might think.

Depending on your business, you may also consider doing a "follower only" offer. These are really easy to post AND test.

Let me tell you a little story about this. I own a coworking space and we opened in April of 2017. We added an additional 1,500 square feet the following year. To celebrate our expansion, we had a party.

One of the people who attended, who I have been friends with online for years asked me, "How are you connected to this business?" My reply was that I OWN it. This serves as a great reminder for me to talk about my business even more!

Let it be an offer for you to do the same.

Ask them how you can help. Are you aware of the best ways you can serve your audience? What are they wondering about? What concerns might they have? What is their pain? You have the opportunity to address any or all of these in your activities on social media.

Ask them if they can help. Are you launching a new product, workshop, or have writer's block? Wondering if your fans will respond? ASK THEM! People love the opportunity to share their opinion and will happily share if you just ask! Try it!

Then, ask them to help you.

Links to your website. Different pages linking to multiple pages on your website helps your SEO and can allow your followers to discover new things about you when they visit. This may be most helpful on LinkedIn but is also beneficial on Pinterest.

Run a social media contest. Do a quick search and you can find some creative ideas for how to run a contest. Please make it easy for people to play along. If you make someone take even five steps to "enter" you might lose them before they even begin.

Poll questions. Polls can be an easy way to drive engagement and are helpful for building your reputation when the poll is directly related to your expertise.

Before and after. There are all sorts of ways to use before and after examples. Web design, weight loss (although this one is a little played out), buildouts of a brick and mortar, graphic design, etc. What before and after ideas can you come up with for yourself?

Caption this. If you took a funny photo in or around your business, try this one.

Get personal. People want to know the people they could be working with, so sharing about who you are outside of your business can be hugely attractive.

- Fun fact
- Hobby or passion
- Pets
- What are you reading?
- What are you watching/bingeing?
- What are you listening to?
- How do you relax?
- What is something on your bucket list?

This week we helped . . . . This is a powerful way to start a sentence. It's another way for you to tell a story around who your clients are and how you support them. For example, "This week we helped a family with a new teenage driver. We added them to the insurance policy and added an umbrella coverage as well." A post like that can spark lots of curiosity and gets the mental Rolodex searching for people we know who might also be in the same place.

Fun ideas

- Vintage advertisements. If you can find ads related to your business, they can get some interesting conversation going. Did you know Coca Cola used to have cocaine in it?

- Fun national holidays. Check the reference section of this book to find holidays that are related to the work you do. There is literally something for everyone.

- Funny pictures/memes/graphics. I love using these on Fridays to go along with #FunnyFriday. I collect these and keep them in a file to make it easy.

Be the expert

- "How-to" videos around your topic
- Live coaching/consulting

- Infographics
- Hacks--solutions they can implement right away.

Solve a simple problem they are likely having, based on the regular challenges your clients have. This helps your prospects see themselves working with you, especially if you are talking about a challenge they are currently experiencing.

Blogs. If you write a regular blog, share posts on your social media, too. Add a comment or two about what they might find when they click through to read.

Make it easy for content creation AND to get responses

All of this "easy engagement" content will benefit you most if it's related to your business. It creates curiosity and starts a conversation.

- This or that? These types of posts can be so great AND fun, which is a bonus for you. Would you rather have X or Y? Add images for effect as well. Example: If you are a caterer or event planner, you could ask, "cake or pie?"

- Fill in the blank. Works well if it makes sense. I've seen horrible examples with multiple blanks to fill in, which aren't as effective as they take a lot of thought. Example: If you are a mortgage broker, "The thing about mortgage I least understand is . . . ." Answers to this could also help you generate more content to clear up confusion.

- What is one word you would use to describe . . . ?

- On a scale of 1-10 . . . . Clearly define what 1 and 10 mean. I used this once and said, "On the scale of 1 to 10, 1 being Eeyore and 10 being Tigger, how excited are you about X?

- What is your favorite X?

- When was the last time you X? (something related to your business)

Ask their opinion. People want to be heard and love expressing their opinions! Ask them what they think. These are people who have already decided they want to engage with your business so if you have a workshop idea, and aren't sure what to call it, ask your fans. One, it creates curiosity, two, there's a whole mess of opinionated people out there, so it can provide for great engagement.

People ideas

If you are part of a non-profit, a company with employees, etc. you can gather some of this information for them as well. It's another way for people to engage with you and your business.

- Behind the scenes. Share pics of your office, employees, team members, customers, etc.

- Photos of you. It goes back to idea that people want to do business with people. They love to see the faces behind the business.

- Your customers

- Your board of directors

- Your members

- Business partners

Let your followers help you create content: (Let them guide and generate content for you.)

- Ask them: How would you search for a service like mine? You might really be surprised about the words they use. This can help you with your messaging down the line.

- What would you do/say? Tell them a short story, maybe with a client challenge, and ask they what they would do in that situation. Example: I have a client who supports people in planning their end-of-life plans. She could say, "Despite her best efforts, one of my private clients has a husband who does NOT want to talk about this topic. What would you do in that situation?"

- Help another parent/client/etc.

Online Communication Beyond Social Media

Blogging is a great tool and can easily be part of the social media marketing discussion. Your blog gives you a better opportunity to tell stories, educate your audience and connect with them on a level deeper than the snippets that other platforms allow.

It is also a great way to keep your website updated, which helps SEO (Search Engine Optimization). When you are blogging, titles are important. Think of the way people search and what they are looking for on a regular basis. Then title your post accordingly.

Speaking of a regular basis . . . How often you blog isn't necessarily as important as being consistent--however that looks for you.

A well-written blog title can determine the difference between your blog being read and spread or sitting in your archives unseen. Use great keywords, make them easier to share and allow readers to comment. Think about what people might be searching for and use that in the title.

One other note about blogs--they don't have to be long. If writing something short works better for you, fantastic! It's better to have regular short posts than the occasional long one.

Invite people to ask you questions and then blog in response to those questions. (This tactic also works for all your social media.)

Contrary to popular myth, **email marketing** is NOT dead.

If you add value and don't sell constantly, e-mail is a great tool for communicating with your clients and potential clients. If every email is a sales offer, though, it may start to look like spam and may not be as effective. Add value first and often, then an ask will be more welcome.

In fact, what's best about email is it is something you actually own! If social media disappeared tomorrow, how would you contact your clients and prospects? If you are actively (and legally) collecting their email addresses, you would be covered.

Subject lines are essential in getting your emails opened and read. This is another great place to create curiosity. What can you title the email that will have your audience wanting more?

RELATIONSHIP

What Is Community?

When talking about community, it can feel like something that is "out there" and therefore not completely tangible.

It's actually a little bit of magic and a whole lot of real-life stories, action, people, etc.

We can look at the dictionary for their definition of community, but that only gives you part of the story.

A community is any group with shared interests, yes that is true. It can also be a shared belief system, the place you live, the church you attend or even the coworking space you are a member of. (wink, wink)

Think about a community--there are young people and old people, white people, brown people, etc. There are people of different family backgrounds, religious beliefs, etc.

There is richness in that kind of diversity.

And since you are creating this community, you get to decide what it looks like.

Here are a few other things I've learned about creating community:

- It can help you solve problems. Two or more brains on the same problem can be so much more helpful than trying to find the solution alone.
- It can give you ideas outside of yourself. If you are an overthinker, or get stuck in your own brain at times, another perspective is priceless.
- It gives you space to be yourself authentically. Community breeds safety to bring your whole self to the table.
- It can bring out the best in you. Sometimes, others being a mirror can be the light we need.
- It can give you more time and energy.

This should become more evident and less magical as we continue.

For now, I would invite you to take a few minutes to think about and/or write down how you feel about the community you are creating.

Case Study, Bri Seeley, BriSeeley.com

Author of *Permission to Leap*, host of the *Success Diaries* Podcast, and founder of the Facebook Group, *The Unapologetic Entrepreneur*

~~~~~

A Community Is a Living Organism

Imagine a call from someone in your community that goes a little like this, "We've never talked, but I've been following you for a year. I've seen everything you've posted. What you just shared . . . I know I'm your next client." That's one of the magical things that happens when you build and foster community, and exactly a call Bri Seeley received in 2019. The woman on the other line didn't even know what Bri's pricing was, she just knew that she was her coach.

Bri has a unique situation as her business has taken some major shifts in the past decades with moves from one coast to the other, and now she is living in Tulsa, Oklahoma.

Her community began with her clothing brand. She was dancing alone to the beat of her own drum, doing her own thing. She was offering different trainings and the people who were buying from her kept asking for more.

Because of that faithful following, she quickly built a community of 2,000 people on Facebook. That group became the basis for her coaching clients and was what got her to her first six-figures in business. She started the group to facilitate a free five-day challenge, and a way to sell another program. Followers continue their membership because they really love her and want to keep getting support from her.

Her community continues to evolve and thrive. They have monthly virtual coworking sessions and a "little posse meetup" where they all get on Zoom so they can see each other's faces. "It's really a space for me to hold and serve all of the women that want my support that just aren't at the place where they can work with me privately or are eligible for any of my programs," Bri said.

It's become so much more than a Facebook group, though. "It's actually a living organism! When the members of the community start supporting each other, and when I don't even have to be in it," she said. They still connect, communicate, and share resources they like. She realizes, "This is something bigger than just me."

The Power of Community (Why Community Matters)

Building your business is so much easier in community. You may not be bought into this idea yet but please stick with me and these ideas. Try some things out, put your heart into it, and then see for yourself.

When you focus your attention on building and creating community, a few key things can happen.

- You are more successful at building advocates and raving fans-- people who without asking will gladly share what you are doing, giving a bigger voice and increased reach for your message.

- You don't see as many downshifts in reach when any social platforms make changes to their algorithms. (These happen all the time.)

- You will experience greater overall success. People can learn and know what you do, give you great referrals and are more apt to share about you.

- You will save time in your marketing efforts. If you have a team involved in the work you are on the planet to do—paid or not-- people who've chosen to join you because they are your champions can save you time by amplifying your efforts.

- You will save money and experience decreased marketing expenses. The time saved comes from no longer paying for boosted or sponsored posts, but rather asking your people to share. You'll see specific examples of what this looks like a bit later.

- You can cut down on the time of your typical buying cycle. When you are focusing on community-building in your marketing, you will attract the right potential consumers and repel those who likely aren't a good fit. In addition, some of the other things we've already shared help with this, too. What it potentially means is by the time people are asking for a phone call with you, you've already shown them exactly who you are and what you do, so are much closer to a yes.

- Everything you are doing on your profiles and connecting with people in real life makes it easy for people to talk ABOUT you! This can mean they show up and comment on social posts, (maybe when you haven't had the chance to reply) better referrals, etc.

You don't have to take my word for it. Here's another case study!

Case Study, Shannon Soriano Greenwood, ReadytoRebelle.com

Founder of *Rule Breaker* Podcast and Rebelle Community

~~~~~

Community IS Her Business

Picture this. You move a lot, so find it challenging to build and maintain relationships. You settle down in a place you are going to call home. Then, you have a baby and experience postpartum depression so severe you walk around the streets of your neighborhood hoping a car would hit you.

That is the beginning of Shannon Soriano Greenwood's story. Over time, she found the support she needed and friends who rallied around her.

While she was going through therapy, she hosted what she called a thank you party. "It was a practice of gratitude," she said. She invited 30 women and wrote them heartfelt notes about why there were important to her and why she wanted them to attend.

She encouraged them to each invite someone who had been there for them during a hard time. And people showed up. "At the time, I thought this is just for me to say thank you, but it was so much more than that."

It only grew from there. She and a group of friends and acquaintances got together to host an event. That quickly expanded into a conference and another conference. Then, they kept hosting events.

In 2018, they launched the Rebelle Community and had 100 members apply right away. They continued to host and throw the kind of events THEY wanted to go to. They believed that if they planned it and no one came, at least *they* would enjoy it. But show up, people did.

One of the things she thinks attracts women to their community is that they don't dumb their message down to the lowest common denominator. "We assume you are actually an intelligent, smart, capable person who just hasn't been given the right tools or opportunity."

She admits her whole business isn't about selling any kind of transformation. "It's all about relationship building," Shannon shared. "I'm in the business of community at this point."

Identify Your Champions and Advocates

"You can be a superstar; you just can't be one alone. What you need is a star system; a constellation of positive, authentic influencers who support each other, reinforce each other, and make each other better."
Shawn Achor, *Big Potential*

You may have heard once or twice (or maybe a thousand times) that you are the sum of the five people you spend the most time with. I understand the thought of this and the idea behind it, AND it's going to take a team or squad or group of more than five for many of us to reach the goals we are aiming toward.

> *"The people we surround ourselves with either raise or lower our standards. They either help us to become the best version of ourselves or encourage us to become lesser versions of ourselves. We become like our friends. No man becomes great on his own. No woman becomes great on their own. The people around them help to make them great.*
>
> *We all need people in our lives who raise our standards, remind us of our essential purpose, and challenge us to become the best version of ourselves."* --Matthew Kelly, *The Rhythm of Life: Living Every Day with Passion and Purpose*

That is the purpose and motivation behind identifying and igniting your champions and advocates.

If you are a marketing department of one, which I imagine many of you are, what kind of difference do you think it could make for your business if you are developing, igniting, nurturing, and building relationships with dozens of people instead of keeping up with the hundreds or thousands you are connected with online?

Let's start by identifying who those champions and advocates might be. Once we do that, we will move forward with what to do with them.

Some of these people may be connections you already have. Others could be people you would LIKE to be your champions and advocates.

Dream a little when you are listing these people. Social can make it easier to connect with some of those on your champions wish list!

Who do you want to spend more time with?

Who is already a fan? Who is that person who calls you with great ideas for YOUR business? Or the ones who always comment or send you referrals?

Who are your favorite clients?

Who are five people you admire?

Who are five leaders in your business community?

Who are the people you always connect with at networking events?

Who are five people who serve the same market as you?

Who are the people your clients hire just before and right after you? (For example, in the case of real estate agents, it could be a contractor, home inspector, or mortgage broker.)

Who are your current referral partners?

Who are your hot prospects or potential business partners? Note: I don't think there is anything nurturing about the word prospect, but I use it here because it's a word that is generally understood.

This list may have 10 people on it, or it may have 50, but I guarantee you it will be WAY easier to have a plan and strategy for keeping in touch with this list than to commit to keeping in touch with ALL your contacts.

Building relationships doesn't happen by accident.

Now that you've identified who these people might be, it's time to do some information gathering.

If it would be helpful for you to have a piece of paper to fill out for each of your champions, you can download one from my website: IgniteYourChampions/book.

- What is their mailing address?
- What are the days that are important to them?

    o When is their birthday?
    o When is their anniversary?
    o Sobriety date?
    o Business anniversary?

- What is their spouse's or partner's name?
- Do they have pets? What are their names?
- Do they have food sensitivities/allergies? This comes in especially handy if you want to bring them treats. It doesn't feel like something special if they can't enjoy what you have given. Remembering food issues can make a world of difference. (Trust me, I'm gluten and dairy free.)
- Where do they play on social media?

- What is their favorite?

    - Candy
    - Treat
    - Movie
    - Quote
    - Actor/Actress
    - Other?

- What is the best way to contact them? (How do THEY like to be contacted?)

    - Text
    - E-mail
    - Phone call
    - Other?

- What is their love language? Love languages can be important because it's valuable to know how THEY want to be treated/loved. For more information, visit 5LoveLanguages.com.

    - Words of affirmation
    - Physical touch
    - Quality time
    - Acts of service
    - Gifts

Some of this information may be easy to find in their profiles, some may mean just asking. This will all make more sense when I talk about how to ignite these people.

For now, know that in our hyper connected world, it's so easy to feel invisible. It's equally easy to remember information about people, showing that you see them.

A little kindness can go a long way, especially when there are many in the marketplace just doing the bare minimum necessary to get by.

This may be a lot to consider, but when you remember small details about people, it can speak volumes of care to them, and it can allow you to thank people personally.

When you have some of this information, it's easier to say thank you in a way that is not only memorable, but unforgettable.

I live in the Seattle area, so a simple thank you tends to include a Starbucks card. It's nice and can easily be forgotten. Thinking of gifts beyond a coffee card is an easy way to surprise and delight!

If you know what they love, you can send a thank you gift they won't quickly forget.

Here is a personal example. I have a friend who loves *Star Wars*. He has also sent me a number of referrals and I wanted a unique way to say thank you. One day, he shared a photo of a Millennium Falcon bottle opener with the word, "want."

Easy peasy. I bought it for him and added a thank you note for his support. Even years later, I imagine that bottle opener is on his fridge.

I have also been the recipient of many of these kinds of unforgettable gifts.

Case Study: Lori Richardson, ScoreMoreSales.com

Author of *She Sells* program and podcast host of *Conversations with Women in Sales*

~~~~~

In Community, One Plus One = More Than Two

How do you know you have a community? Lori Richardson's answer is simple and powerful. "People show up when you need them. They respond when you ask them. They invite others to join in."

She is in several communities of sales professionals that are made up of experts, influencers, sales experts, "wannabes," up-and-comers and tons of salespeople and sales managers/leaders. Most of them found each other on LinkedIn by posting updates that led to responses. Over time, a huge community was built.

"All of the communities are interwoven into how I do business. I'd be nothing much without them," she said.

Here's what is most amazing, many of these women could be competitors. They all have their own businesses doing sales or helping other companies sell. "So, we are doing the same things," she said, "but some are authors, speakers, trainers, consultants, some work with big organizations and others are very niche."

When people first come in, sometimes they are reluctant to participate, but once they do, they see "the power of leveraging each other."

Lori calls herself a connector and people collector, which means presenting opportunities to collaborate. She knows she doesn't have to do things on her own, but rather, she "gets a lot of enjoyment out of doing something with somebody."

She shared a brilliant example. She was recently approached to be on the cover of a top sales magazine and someone at that magazine reached out to interview her. She asked if she could, instead, pick the person to be interviewed. She chose an up-and-comer from her women's sales pros group, which gave her some additional visibility.

You never know what you can create when you bring people together. "Yes, and it's always better. You know, it's like one plus one equals more than two," she said, "something bigger."

Ignite Your Champions and Advocates

"Customers don't want to be caught; they want to be courted."
Denise Duffield-Thomas, *Chillpreneur*

50+ ways to connect online and off

Connecting with people doesn't have to take a ton of time when you are focused and strategic and not trying to be everything to everyone. That's exhausting! Can you connect with everyone? Absolutely not! It is much easier to focus on a targeted group of people you want to stay more connected with for any number of reasons. They can be advisors, prospects, partners, and potential collaborators. Spending time on these relationships will give you the opportunity to explore what's possible.

One important item to note about this list--you won't be able to use the same tactics with everyone. This will become obvious very quickly. Usually, a multi-media approach will have maximum impact.

Also important to note--these ideas are not about adding to the hustle. You will find some of these suggestions take seconds while others may take more thought and time. Pick a few you love and that really work for you or for your champions!

Ways to grow your relationship on social media

If they have a blog, try these tactics:

- Comment on their blog post directly. It is easy when writing a blog to feel like no one is reading it. Take a few moments to read their blog and write a thoughtful, even if it's short, response. An added benefit to this is a backlink to your website which can help you with SEO.

- Share their blog post, especially if it is relevant to your audience. If you share it on Facebook or LinkedIn, be sure to tag them in the post. You can also share it on Pinterest if that is something you use, which is also really great for SEO.

- Offer to trade guest blog posts. Again, this will be most effective if you have a similar audience. Trading blog posts is a great way to serve each other's audience AND grow your network. It's a win/win!

I hope you have a podcaster or two on your list. There are a few tried and true ways to their hearts.

- Subscribe to their podcast on whatever platform you use. The top two platforms for this are Spotify and iTunes.

- Write them a review. I've heard podcasters refer to reviews as currency. It helps their content get found by more people when there are positive reviews.

- If they have a call to action, act on it. Many podcasters are asking for engagement on specific platforms, so go there and do what they are asking.

- Share a specific episode on your page and say why you are sharing it.

LinkedIn is a great platform for sharing business-related content. It's especially nice during our current political climate. It is understood that LinkedIn is a business-to-business platform and while many use it for their job searches, there are also many relevant conversations and connections happening.

- Write them a recommendation. When writing, consider making it a combination of their work skills and part of their personality. Both are valuable.

- Comment on their status update. LinkedIn can be a great relationship building tool when you spend time commenting, and not just liking. Create and add to the conversation.

- Follow their company page. This can be especially helpful when it comes to the people you are building to be champions. When you follow and then regularly comment on their company page, it increases their reach and your visibility.

- If you are looking to connect with specific industry leaders and add them to your champions list, you can join groups they are active in to start a conversation with them. Participate in discussions they are involved in. Once you do this, it may become appropriate to send a connection request.

Instagram is a powerful platform that can be filled with cotton candy content, but there are many in the space who are using it to share mini-blog posts and sharing vulnerability and authenticity in ways that are super effective. While the tendency might be to go through your feed and double tap photos to like, Instagram is shifting up their algorithms to reward content that creates conversation.

- Make a thoughtful comment on their post. It doesn't have to be long, but there are a lot of bots on IG and making a relevant comment is always appreciated.

- Share about them or share their content to your stories. Always be sure to tag them!

- Send them a direct message in response to an Instagram post or story. It can be easy to feel like you are talking to no one. Sending a DM helps them know someone is listening.

Facebook is still the largest social media platform and while the demographics and usage have shifted, Facebook as a platform isn't going anywhere. Nearly a billion and a half people visit every day. It also still leads the way for most monthly active users.

- Comment on their Facebook business page. This is one of the easiest and most effective ways to support your friends in business. Commenting on their page keeps their content in your news feed too, which makes it easier to continue to engage, making those comments and their content visible to more people.

- Share content from their Facebook business page. This is a simple way to introduce your community to the other amazing people you know.

- Invite five of your friends to like their Facebook business page. What a huge service you can do for your connections--to personally invite others to like their page. Make sure it's relevant. For example, it isn't necessarily helpful for me (in Seattle, WA) to like an attorney's page in New Mexico.

- Share their Facebook business page on your timeline. When you share their page, tell a personal story or provide a recommendation for WHY your friends might like their page.

- Write a recommendation on their business page. Make it specific and personal for maximum impact!

- If you find an article, image or meme you think they might be interested in, either share it on their timeline or send as a private message. Everyone loves to be thought of and it will confirm that you know their interests.

You might have noticed there is no mention of reactions. Reacting to a post never started or sustained a conversation. If you really want to have impact AND be memorable, take a moment to engage and comment. It's a simple way to add to the conversation.

Pinterest isn't one of the most active sites based on average users, but it is a powerhouse for organic reach and SEO. In fact, it's the third largest search engine after Google and YouTube.

Pinterest isn't necessarily the place to comment on content, but it's a great place to share things your champions have created, such as websites, books, blogs, etc.

Simplicity Solution: Add Pinterest extension to your Chrome browser That makes it easy to share info to your Pinterest account about your champions.

- Create a board with all your champions and advocates. I have one called "People you should know." It's a great acknowledgement of my peers and it's a nice boost for THEIR SEO.

- Create a board with great blog posts they have written. Include their name and the title of their blog in the description.

- Create a board with books you recommend. I imagine a few or more of your champions have written books. Add them to this list!

Twitter has seen some shifts recently, but many of your connections are likely still using it. Especially when it comes to influencers, media, and authors, they are active and it's easy to connect with them there.

- Retweet their content. If their content is relevant to your audience, share it.

- Reply to their tweet. While there are character limits, it's still possible to connect and have conversations.

- Add them to a list. Lists are a great way to listen to and connect with specific people on Twitter. I used to have lists created for "people I adore" and "awesomesauce." Because I've named my lists this way, it has meant the people I've added tend to follow back. When you first add someone to a list, they receive a notification and it's an additional way to leverage your relationships.

Write them an online review. This one might be a bit trickier as it might take some research to find out where they like to receive reviews.

- Do they use Yelp, Houzz, Angi? (Formerly Angie's List) Write a review in the appropriate place. Or are they on Google, Facebook, and Alignable? It seems new places where businesses gather are always popping up. If you are unsure about where they might like a review, just ask. They will be more than happy to tell you!

- If they are an author, write them an Amazon book review. When a book on Amazon has a certain number of book reviews, it means their book is more likely to show up in search and listed as a "like search." Writing a review for their book can be a huge boost.

- Subscribe to their YouTube Channel. The number of subscribers someone has gives them more reach, authority AND can give them the power to monetize their channel.

Offline activities can be even more effective. Let's look at ways to grow your business relationships socially, like with your champions and advocates. That's what this is all about.

- Make a personal phone call. For some of you, this might be a regular part your business anyway. Many are exchanging texts and emails instead of actual live conversations. That's what can make those phone calls more powerful and memorable. They key to making this effective is calling for no reason--this is not about asking for a referral. You need to build the relationship to earn the right to ask for that.

- Send a handwritten note/greeting card. Personal, hand-written cards seem to be a lost art. Have cards and stamps on hand to make it easy to send a quick note. When you send a card, do NOT include your business card or a sticker that says, "Oh, by the way, I love referrals." When you add those elements, your greeting card might now be seen as a marketing piece. The same is true if you share a happy birthday graphic on social media that has your logo on it. Not good.

- Share an article with them. Did you read an article in the newspaper, business journal or magazine that made you think of someone? Cut it out and mail it to them. Taking it back super old-school. If you find it online, send it in an email.

- Set up a coffee date with no agenda. Real live, face-to-face interaction is still very powerful and effective. Make the time! You won't be disappointed. To be clear, it's not possible to meet in person with everyone! Focus on your champions and advocates.

- When you set up the coffee date, invite along a third person who would be a great connection.

- Set up a Zoom chat. Geography may prevent in-person meetings. Zoom is a great alternative.

- Buy someone lunch. Even the busiest of us still needs to eat.

- Schedule a "walk and talk." Exercise, fresh air and conversation. What a great combination!

- Send a small gift in the mail. Keep notes of those special things people like and surprise them with goodies in the mail. If you want to send a gift, but don't know what they like, look at their social media profiles.

- Stop by their office with a treat--whatever that might look like for them.

- Send them an encouraging text. It can be a great way to supplement other communications.

- Ask them for advice. I don't know about you, but I love it when people ask me for advice. It makes people feel good to know you trust them enough to reach out. The key to this is to be sure to honor what is advice and what you might want to be paying them for.

- Host an event, small or large--it's a great way to connect. This is a fantastic way for the people you know to meet one another!

- Show up at an event they are hosting. Holding events can be challenging, so having a friendly face in the audience is always helpful.

- Show up at an event they are attending. This seems self-explanatory but already having a buddy at an event can be helpful at breaking the ice and meeting new people.

- Offer to help/support them at an event they are hosting. Holding events can be very stressful with lots of little details. Offering your support can be like a breath of fresh air!

- Register and PAY for their event.

- Subscribe to their email newsletter. For your champions, subscribing to their newsletter is a simple way to keep up with what they have going on.

- Reply to their email newsletter. If they are asking a question or provided you value, let them know by replying!

- Cohost a Facebook or Instagram Live session with them. This is an example of sharing your audience. It's a great way to introduce your champions to your other connections.

- Ask them what support they need right now. This can be a huge boost to them AND you. Sometimes, just the simple act of offering support can be a big deal. You are letting them know you are thinking of them, etc. Of course, if they ask for something, you should be willing to honor that.

For these to be effective in the long run, there must be no agenda. This needs to be honest and heartfelt giving, with no expectations. People are smart enough to see through giving that is selfish in nature.

Most of these are free or very low cost. What can you do today to surprise and delight your champions and advocates? Those little things can be the difference between completely ordinary and truly unforgettable.

When you are regularly spending time nurturing and caring for your network, you are making deposits into their emotional bank accounts. When you spend that time, it's much easier to request a withdrawal.

The Platinum Rule. You know the golden rule--do unto others as you would have them do unto you. The problem with that rule and igniting your champions is that this isn't about you--it's about them. That means it could be necessary to test to see what works best for them. Do they love personal phone calls? That's good information to have. Do they hate texting? Again, super helpful.

The platinum rule is: "Do unto others as *they* would want done to *them,"* according to Dave Kerpen, author of *The Art of People.* He says, "The Golden Rule, as great as it is, has limitations, since all people and all situations are different. When you follow the Platinum Rule, however, you can be sure you're actually doing what the other person wants done and assure yourself of a better outcome."

Champion pro tip: Set up Google alerts for your champion's name and/or business. You will get notified when their name shows up online and then get to be one of the first to acknowledge them for their mention or accomplishment, etc.

We've all heard that the definition of insanity is doing the same thing and expecting different results. Doing what everyone else is willing to do keeps you and your business at the status quo. To be remarkable, memorable, and even effective in your efforts, there are times you must be willing to do what others may not. This list is short and simple and can help make you not just memorable, but unforgettable.

So I ask you, what are you willing to do to really make an impact in your relationships and business? There are so many people settling for less, it doesn't take much to stand out above the crowd.

Why Ignite Your Champions?

Think about this, would you rather be a pebble in a lake or a boulder in a puddle? Which one makes the bigger impact?

Pebbles are what most people are throwing around when it comes to their marketing. Again, going back to the spray and pray approach. They may be playing small or have messaging that is easily forgettable. They have profiles everywhere and post in dozens of groups on a regular basis, but they don't pay attention enough to any of them to have an impact. Those are the pebbles. In the big ocean that is the online space or business industry in general, the splash from a tiny rock could easily be missed.

Now, think about tossing a boulder into a puddle. You wouldn't be able to miss the impact on the puddle.

Maybe a better analogy would be the snowball rolling downhill. When you are growing your relationships and building community, that ball of snow continues to grow and can have a remarkable impact on whatever is in its way.

Igniting your champions allows you to scale your relationship-building. It's no longer about who you know, although that plays into it, but it's about who they know and who they know and so on.

Focusing on community allows you to convert online relationships into offline friendships. And better yet, allows those relationships to become paying clients. More on that shortly.

Your champions will not only want you to succeed, but they will take action to help when you let them know you are in need. If you need help or support, you have to ask. They won't be able to GUESS what you need.

Let me share a story that brings this idea into focus.

> I started InSpark Coworking in April 2017. It was a business model that was completely foreign to me (brick and mortar with a membership component). Looking back, it is one of the most challenging things I have ever done in my business life.
>
> Most of the time, I felt like I was failing. We were growing, yes, but not nearly as the speed that would allow me to do important things, like pay rent in a timely manner, if at all.
>
> It was April 2019 and this struggle felt impossible. And I felt alone.
>
> I was on the phone, sharing my story with a friend and champion. I will never forget what she said on the phone that day. "Tracey, you have people who know you and love you and they don't know you need help." She told me I needed to ask for help. Duh.
>
> I did ask for help. And my community delivered. That was my first $10K revenue month.
>
> While the financial part of this story is important, what became more important was the reminder to ask for help and the power at my fingertips in my community.

I promise you, most of your friends who are in businesses themselves are too wrapped up in what they have going on to always know what's going on with you.

If you need help, you just have to ask.

In fact, you may want to keep a running list of what support you are looking for. As you are actively growing and engaging a community, you will likely get asked more often what kind of help you currently need. Having an answer keeps the win/win in action.

Create a Listening Strategy

There are a couple great ways to listen on social media and both are equally important.

First, it is important to listen to the people who are responding to you, those who are actively engaging on your posts. The number of businesses who don't respond to people on their pages has always been very high at 90 percent. Just acknowledging their comments puts you in the top 10 percent.

I also believe rewarded behavior gets repeated and since I want people to continue to comment on my posts, I want them to know I see what they wrote and am grateful.

In addition to this, comments are a great way to show the algorithm (the magical math equation behind how your content gets delivered) that this is popular, and they will deliver it to more people. Bonus!

If you can take just a few minutes every day to check on your profiles to find and respond to new comments, you will be well on your way to building great rapport and community.

Social media is a powerful listening tool. That might sound counterintuitive, but with so many others sharing and sharing, when you commit to taking time to read, listen and hear, there is unique opportunity for impact.

The second way to listen on social media is to create a strategy for HOW you pay attention to the champions and advocates you've already identified.

You can't listen to everyone, but you can listen to those you have chosen. This might include creating a spreadsheet with their social links, adding them to a favorites list, or creating specific connection groups to help. (These are features on Facebook and LinkedIn.) You might find a system/structure unique to you as well.

Practical Ignition in 30 Minutes (or Less) Per Day

"Success is not just about how creative or smart or driven you are, but how well you are able to connect with, contribute to, and benefit from the ecosystem of people around you."
Shawn Achor, *Big Potential*

Now that you've identified your list of champions and advocates, maybe you have a CRM (Customer Relationship Manager) program you use to stay in touch, or for now, it might be a notebook or a spreadsheet. Either way is OK, but having some way to track this activity will benefit you in the long run.

If you are interested in making a game of this, I created an Ignite Your Champions Bingo board that you can download by visiting NYNBingo.com.

If a game isn't your thing, we've already talked about practical actions you can take on a regular basis to ignite your champions. But what does this look like in reality?

Let's talk about some potential schedules for something like this.

Set aside time in your calendar to take action!

In my group coaching program, we have monthly Champions Coworking time. We gather on Zoom and each take time to nurture our networks, whatever that looks like for each individual person.

Here are some things you can block out in your calendar:

- Monthly time to write birthday cards.

- Weekly times to engage on social media.

- Weekly times to check in on LinkedIn, Facebook, or Instagram-- wherever your champions are posting their content.

- Monthly time to visit their blog posts, comment and share to Pinterest (if applicable)

- Weekly time to make phone calls.

- Weekly time to send texts.

- Monthly time to schedule lunch meetings, register for events, etc.

The possibilities for this are endless, but I'm sure you know success is scheduled, so if this doesn't get on your calendar, it might not happen. Or is that just me?

Another item that will bring ease into your connecting is creating scripts and templates you can use over and over.

For the longest time, I made this hard for myself. I wrote and rewrote every connection request, reconnection note, and private message.

I now keep a list of copy and paste blurbs that I use for connecting and reconnecting with people online or for sending out similar private messages to individual people.

I often ask myself, "How can I bring ease into this activity?" It's a great question to find new ways to simplify.

Another idea I'm playing with is having a regular champions check-in. This would be a time dedicated to checking in with myself around these activities.

Here are some regular questions you can ask yourself.

- What were your wins from connecting in the last week/month?

- Who did you acknowledge/thank/support this week?

- Who did you connect with this week? What support do they currently need?

- Who needs to hear from you in the coming week?

- Who has a special day coming up?

- Who did you ask for help or support? (Do they also need a thank you?)

Asking these questions on a regular basis will make a habit out of igniting your champions.

Build Community on Your Personal Profile

When I am out, people often comment to me about how much they love what I post on social media. It's not hard to create content that gets people to say that. It's about creating curiosity and showing a genuine interest in others.

It can also serve as a way for YOU to get to know your community and potential champions.

It's easy to brainstorm ideas, but here are a few questions to ask that can start the flow. Many of these questions will also help you in getting to know your Champions and Advocates.

- What is your love language?
- What was your favorite subject in school?
- What is something you would tell yourself if you were just starting your business?
- What is your favorite business book?
- What are three words other people use to describe you?
- What are your top three core values?
- Do you have a secret talent? What is it?
- What is one thing you are grateful for?
- What always puts you in a good mood?
- What's your favorite song right now?
- How would you describe what you do to a five-year-old?
- What is a talent you wish you had?

- If you could have any superpower, what would it be?
- Who would you like to have dinner with tonight? (alive or dead)
- What is your favorite inspirational movie?
- Who is someone you would like to meet right now? Why?
- What was the last book you read?
- What is your favorite candy?
- When you feel stuck, what do you do?
- What is your favorite form of self-care?
- What TV show are you currently watching?
- What would you say is the most important characteristic of a great leader?
- Who is a leader you admire? Why?
- Do you serve on a non-profit board?
- How would you describe the work you do in five words or less?
- What is one goal you have for this month?
- Share what you do but do it badly. (This one can be a lot of fun!)

What are some other questions that come to mind for you?

Conversation Starters Beyond "How Are You?"

When attending a networking event, it's easy to get stuck in "how are you" type small talk that isn't very effective for building relationship or supporting one another as you are growing your business.

Asking unique questions is another way to create curiosity about who you are and what you do.

Next time you are at an event, try some of these questions and see what magic might result.

- Who are you looking for an introduction to right now?

- What is the biggest challenge you are having in your business right now?

- What kind of support do you need right now?

- What do you love most about the work you do?

- Who are your favorite people to work with?

- What do you love most about attending this event?

- What kinds of businesses make great connections for you?

- What are you working on right now that has you excited?

- What do you love most about owning your own business?

- What support are you looking for in your business right now? What is the best way for me to refer clients to you?

- If you were starting over, what piece of advice would you give yourself?

- What win are you celebrating right now?

- What was your intention in coming to this event?

- What do your clients get from working with you?

- What is your business superpower?

- What kinds of partnerships are you currently looking for?

ENGAGEMENT

Get Your Champions to Share Your Content

I hear many people sharing their frustration with Facebook and decreased reach of social media in general. "What do you mean only 12 people saw that post?" Can you relate?

I have a solution you may want to try before throwing in the towel, or before you opt to pay for any promotion.

When you work toward creating a community in your social media space (and in life), you have built-in people who already appreciate you and your business. You can activate these people to your advantage! Sometimes, it's as simple as asking for help.

Here is the idea: If you have a special event coming up, a great new blog post, a special you are offering, (hold on to your hats) . . .

ASK YOUR CHAMPIONS TO SHARE IT!

I know. Mind blowing, right?

Send a private message to five of your champions and ask them to share-- in private or direct messages, of course. Make it as easy as possible for people to pass information along and they likely will. Send the link to the original post. That allows them to click directly to it to comment and share.

This works for several reasons.

- It's FREE! (Bonus!)

- If they are your champions and advocates (and you've already been making deposits into their emotional bank accounts), they will do it AND they will likely be sharing with YOUR ideal client/customer. (Birds of a feather flock together.)

- When they share, it will usually come with a testimonial--which makes it SUPER powerful.

And sharing is contagious. You might ask five people to share, but in the end, many more might share it. I have seen this in action over and over!

Chances are this approach will get your specific post more reach than a boosted or sponsored post anyway! Better reach without spending money seems like another win/win!

If you are part of an organization or non-profit, ask your board, employees, or volunteers to share! If you are in a networking group, sharing each other's content is the easiest way to support your fellow members. More about this in a moment.

Please, please, please, TRY THIS. You might be pleasantly surprised by the results!

Amplify Your Organizations by Sharing

Can I get on a soapbox for a moment?

I have been a part of quite a few organizations over the years--business associations, chambers of commerce, non-profits and the like. And honestly, if the members of the board or organization would commit only 30 minutes per week to support the other members, it could change everything!

Let's think about the networks you are already a part of:

- Networking groups
- BNI (Business Network International)
- Chambers of commerce
- Fraternal organizations
- Non-profits
- Churches
- Alumni organizations
- Social clubs and groups

Imagine for a moment what could be possible if everyone in these groups were spending time every day amplifying the members of said group. This is not JUST about multiplication of results; it's about creating community. The increased reach is an added benefit.

Practically, here is what that looks like.

You are a member of a non-profit board that runs local events to support your cause. If every board member would share about the event, invite friends and comment on the posts on the non-profit's social media platforms, the reach for that event would increase exponentially. That elevates the event and the non-profit overall.

If you are part of a networking group, you could do the same thing.

If everyone in the group would commit 30 minutes a week to comment and engage with each other's content, the results would be tangible and measurable almost immediately.

Important to note—I've already mentioned I believe rewarded behavior gets repeated. When someone comments on your post, comment back. It's nice for your "fan" to get the acknowledgement and more comments means the post will be seen by more people.

Bonus tip: Schedule time for your group to write online reviews for one another. That's a fantastic way to amp up the effectiveness of a group and everyone's business reputation.

Create Community in Groups

Groups can be a fantastic way to grow your audience, expertise, and community.

Should you join other groups or start your own? Maybe both.

You can implement some simple techniques to make groups more effective both as an owner and as a member. This is most applicable to groups on Facebook, but the advice is beneficial for any online group you are a part of.

As a member:

- Engage on a regular basis. Many groups have daily prompts that make it easy to get involved.

- Add and give value. Doing this without selling will also create curiosity.

- Offer yourself as a resource. Sometimes, there will be questions asked where you ARE the expert. This is a great opportunity to show a teeny bit of what working with you might look like.

- Don't just drop your link and ditch. I have witnessed so many people doing this. They have an upcoming event, so they visit each of their FB groups and share about themselves and what is coming up, then leave, never spending any time in the group getting to know that community. In cases like this, it appears they are checking "marketing" off on their to do list--and then scratch their heads wondering why no one responds.

As the group owner and moderator:

- Provide regular prompts to get to know the people in your group.

- Add and give value. Since this is your group, you have a huge opportunity here.

- Be a resource.

- Set clear guidelines for the group. This is helpful for the members in the short term and will be beneficial to you in the long term.

- Ask for group members' emails and let them know you are adding them to your list.

If you are starting your own group, send private messages with personal invites. It will make a difference in getting your group to grow.

Make a Difference for Your Bottom Line

Building expertise with authenticity, online and off, is where all the work you've done up until now comes together.

I think I have talked about the touchy-feely part of creating community enough at this point. While I believe community changes the world, money is also a part of that change.

Can community make a difference for your bottom line? Heck yes! In fact, if it doesn't, something needs to change.

How does this happen?

Cash flow from your community doesn't happen overnight, but rather over time.

Relationships evolve and change the same way.

Creating community online and off allows you to take a cold market, warm it up through igniting and make it hot!

If this hasn't happened for you, you might need to go back and check some things out. Is your messaging clear? Are you making deposits into your champions emotional bank accounts? Really?

I have a story for this too.

> I have a connection who used to regularly mark "interested" on events I was hosting on Facebook. They never came to an event. Just said they were interested.

> Fast forward a couple months, and I get a message from this person that says something to the effect of, "Well, I've been marking "interested" for all your events and that helps your events get seen by more people, so now can you do something for me?" WHAT? They weren't helping me in any way (that was obvious to me) and then asked for help. It didn't line up.

Community can allow you to accelerate relationships. In cases like the story above, it can also bring something to a screeching halt.

Here are a few thoughts to ponder that might support you in cash creation through your community:

- Marketing is about lead generation; sales is about converting those leads. All the marketing in the world can't drive revenue if you aren't making a sale.

- Ask for what you want when it comes to sales. If you don't ask for the sale, you can't expect them to buy.

- Stop nurturing them and tell them you have a solution. It's easy to get stuck in the give, give, give rhythm. You have something that will be of benefit to them, but you have to say so.

- Every click is an invitation to a conversation. I heard this recently on a coaching call with Tara Newman of the Bold Profit Academy and it was a great shift for me. When people engage with your content, treat it like an invitation. Send a private message, start a conversation and be open to possibility.

Case Study: Debbie Page, DebbiePage.com

Founder of *Women's Business Profit Lab* Facebook Group

~~~~~

Community Leads to Cash Flow

Why can't you just have a group for the sake of building community? This is a question Debbie Page asked herself as she was launching her business. You see, the advice of the day was to build a big group, launch a thing and have a staff. She knew there was a better way. In this case, her way.

She started the Women's Business Profit Lab to invite women in who wanted to talk about money. "Cash flow and profitability are sacred things, and they are scary to talk about," she said. She knows these are important topics and recognized people were scared to talk about them for fear of judgment.

Vulnerable conversations are the result of the space Debbie has created. She offers weekly trainings about cash flow, profitability, and other topics. She has been a business owner for over 25 years and understands that lots of people have done a lot of nice and good things for her. It's her way of giving back--not as part of a funnel or whatever. "It's just a good thing to do."

Those discussions became even more important during the COVID-19 pandemic time period as many wondered about the future of their business during and following the pandemic.

People care. That's how she knows what she is creating. "A community shows up with ideas and resources. They care about your success; they care about the success of the people they are referring." When they ask you how you are doing, they also know when you are trying to pull one over on them and they notice when you go missing.

Debbie continues to foster her community by doing "random acts of kindness for no particular reason." She clarified, "If you are doing something because it's an angle, it's never going to work. If you are doing something because you really care, it will always work." She added that it may take longer, it may be bumpier, but it will always work.

How has this community affected her bottom line? A staggering two-thirds of her current clients were referred at some point by someone in the Profit Lab.

In addition, because she is clear in her messaging, adds value through her weekly trainings and prompts in her group, it means she is the first person people think of when someone else is looking for a business coach who talks about money and business.

What You Measure Matters

It's so easy as a business owner to jump on the newest trends on social media. But are they effective for YOUR ideal audience? That is a question many business owners could be asking, and based on what I'm seeing online, I am guessing they are not.

I treat all my marketing like one big experiment. It makes the activities a little more fun and a lot less daunting AND it allows me to share what's working (or not) with the people around me.

It is very simple to test--and that is what this chapter is about.

Hustle culture makes us believe we should be doing all the things all the time. Taking time to measure what really matters can save you time and long-term heartache and headache.

Here are a few options you might not be considering:

To automate or not to automate. Automation tools can make it easier to get your message out to multiple platforms. There is research that shows them to be effective for some platforms and less effective for others. Look at your insights and analytics to decide for yourself.

How to test:

Use your automation tool to post as usual. But sprinkle in some native (direct to the platform) posts. Do this for a couple weeks and look at the results. What is the reach of the posts from the scheduler compared to the native posts? Then, adjust accordingly if needed.

What time of day is best to post? Ask the internet and you will get dozens of different opinions about the answer to that question. The answer lies in YOUR audience and not the experts! Pay attention to your audience and the weather and world events. For example, in the Seattle area, it's nearly a waste of time to post on Sunday afternoons during football season--unless you are talking about the Seahawks.

Know your audience and where they live and when they spend time on social media. If most of your audience is on the West Coast (and so are you) you may not want to post at 6 a.m. since they are likely still in bed and not looking at their social media. If your ideal client is a mom, you may not want to post during the dinner hour.

How to test:

Vary the times of day you post and check the reach. It's also important to share that every time I've ever found a pattern, the random 9 p.m. post could also get engagement. It does start to feel random, but this is a tip that can help you a ton.

How often should you be posting on your page? Again, the "experts" are all over the place on this. It used to be that more was better, but that is shifting as people change the way they are consuming content and spending their time on social media.

How to test:

Take a screen shot of your insights and then test. Post once a day, twice a day, or three times a week. It doesn't really matter what frequency you choose but be consistent. That's MOST important. Then, watch your page reach or insights. Does increasing your number of posts help your reach? That will be a good indicator.

What kind of content is the most effective? Facebook likes variety, so posting different kinds of posts is important. What does that mean? Photos, text only, links, videos. They could and likely should be part of your content strategy. Instagram content seems to benefit from telling short stories instead of just cheesy motivational quotes.

How to test:

This is the hardest one of all! I hear people say all the time, "I post and no one ever comments." Sometimes, I look and see they aren't commenting because you aren't asking a question. Facebook's algorithm likes content that gets comments! (and shares!) and aren't as focused on what gets likes. This one may take the longest to test, but experiment with different things. Also, it's important to note that even if no one comments, it is making a difference. There are a lot of people who simply watch and listen on social media. So even if they never acknowledge you, they are there and likely paying attention. Even if no one is commenting, it does all benefit your search engine results.

Are people visiting your website or event listings as a result of what you post? This one isn't as much a test as a report you can check. Look at your Google analytics. Are people visiting your website from your social media platforms? I would be willing to bet that if you adjust the first three items in this post, you will see better results in your analytics.

I know this is a lot to pay attention to. Slight shifts can make the world of difference!

When you find what's working, keep doing it!

Case Study: Nikki Rausch, YourSalesMaven.com

Author of *Six-Word Lessons on Influencing with Grace, Buying Signals*, and *The Selling Staircase* and podcast host of *Sales Maven with Nikki Rausch,* and founder of the *Sales Maven Society*

~~~~~
Paying Attention Is Paying off

Nikki Rausch started the Sales Maven Society in 2017 and her initial goal was to grow it to 200 members and generate $10K in revenue per month. While it took longer to grow it than she initially hoped, she noticed some remarkable things happening.

While this is a paid group, members also started signing up for other offerings from Nikki. In addition to signing up for more services, "they bring other people into the group too," she said, "so what it contributes now to my bottom line is significant." Her guess was that the Society members account for more than 60 percent of her business revenue.

Her community has shown up not just for themselves, but for each other. She shared, "I know I have community in two ways, one because they show up and participate, engaging with each other. And what really cements it for me is I have people connecting in my group and then taking that relationship outside of the group." They are working together, collaborating, and even becoming friends.

The Sales Maven Society is a space that provides an opportunity for people to learn selling skills, and it's also an opportunity for then to have a safe space to ask vulnerable questions, because of the culture Nikki has created. The community is made up of people of all levels of experience--some way ahead and some behind, but all open and willing to give suggestions and solutions, along with Nikki offering support.

Nikki has been paying extra close attention to how and when she is making offers, and where sales are coming from, etc. And that attention is paying off. She talks about "pouring gasoline" on what's working. For example, she realized being a guest on podcasts was a great way to generate leads, so she poured gas on that and upped that part of her marketing.

One significant story she shared was about someone who heard Nikki on a podcast. They reached out to schedule a call with her to find out ways to work with her. Between scheduling and the time of the call, this person joined the Sales Maven Society and bought a Masterclass. Then, when this person got on the call with Nikki, they also signed up to be a VIP client. That all happened within a 10-day span.

Nikki and her team are always actively looking for ways to engage their community. From a recent Member Appreciation Month to member-offered trainings and regular connection calls. "It's all about engagement, community and retention," Nikki said.

Just Comment!

For best effectiveness, stop clicking like.

I get it. We are all busy. And that can lead to a mindless scroll through Facebook, Instagram or LinkedIn to pass the time, or continue to avoid the task that is nagging at us.

It's so easy to do this and click like, react, or hit the double tap.

The problem is it is another thing that makes you forgettable.

It takes less than a second to click "like" or react to a post. And chances are your individual action won't be seen because of the nature of each platform, since likes and reactions are all aggregated. For example, you and 39 other people . . . .

Commenting does a few things for you. If you are igniting your champions on social media, it helps your name be seen by them, and by other people who are connected with them.

If you comment, it doesn't take a lot of time, but ALWAYS gets noticed. Even if your comment is a one-word response, it shows you took the time to say something. It allows people to see your name on a regular basis-- another way to stay top of mind. But more than that, commenting helps THEIR content reach more people because the algorithms see that their content is popular and will therefore deliver it to more people. That's a gift to them, from you.

This is another reason it's important to keep your information up to date on all your current profiles. When you are commenting, there is an opportunity for those comments to create curiosity in others that may have them checking out your profiles!

Don't Buy into the Lies

Oh, there are so many lies--you have to be on every platform. You need to friend/connect with as many people as possible. You need a "list" in the thousands to be successful and build a six-figure or seven-figure business.

Do you need to grow a huge audience? The answer is, it depends. Are you selling a $10 item? Then, yes, a large audience will be beneficial.

In most industries, a smaller following will benefit you greatly, especially when you keep your focus on building community and fostering relationships.

Vanity metrics (number of followers, likes, reach, etc.) don't mean anything, really. When you first start your Facebook page, Twitter or Instagram account, it's easy to get obsessed with watching the count. "How many likes or followers do I have today?" Those numbers will grow as you provide great content and work toward building a community around your business.

That isn't to say those numbers aren't helpful. They are. They can help you decide what content is most helpful to those people who follow you. Depending on how they engage can help you know what they like and what they don't and allow you to shift accordingly.

Focus on quality instead of quantity. This isn't a race to get as many likes and followers as possible. I would rather have 1,000 fans who love my brand and are advocates than 10,000 who clicked like just because. In fact, studies have shown that the bigger the numbers, the more challenging it is to get that engagement you are looking for.

Here are some other lies you might have been sold:

- You have to hustle and grind to be successful. Absolute BS. My current business focus is all around ease and joy, and it's making what I'm doing more fun for me, which allows for more impact with the people I'm working with.

- You have to create content every day for every platform. Creating new content every day is a trap! What if you could create one to 200 pieces of content that you could use forever? How would that change your life? Stay tuned!

- Your market is saturated. I totally hear this one. Considering I know at least 30 Real Estate agents, this might be true. But dig a little deeper and you will find information beyond what appears to be saturation. While it may be 30 agents, they each have a different kind of client they work with, areas of the city they work in, and all sorts of other things they do that make them unique. This is part of what makes your messaging SO important. If you sound like everyone else, you won't stand out.

Make It Easy for People to Hire You

This seems simple enough, but you might be surprised.

Imagine your PERFECT customer is ready to work with you. They heard you on a podcast, get your emails, follow you on social media or however you have become top-of-mind for them. They visit your Facebook or Instagram page and can't find your website or phone number. If they are determined, they might even do a quick search for you. They have found your web page, but there is no phone number, no pricing, and no obvious way for them to reach out to you right now.

What do you think they might do next? I've got an idea and it likely doesn't include hiring you at all.

Make it easy for people to contact you and hire you!

Make sure all your profiles are filled out completely.

Make sure they match, at least in a way that lets them know they are in the right place. If the colors and images aren't somewhat consistent, a buyer might not know they have found you.

Include your freaking phone number! This one has baffled me. So many businesses don't have phone number listed anywhere.

List your prices on your website. Time is a precious commodity. If I don't have your pricing in my budget, I want to know that before I take time with you on a phone call, etc. If you aren't comfortable listing your price, use "Prices start at $_____" to give a prospect an idea. I am aware there are very different and opposing views about this topic. I also know many people won't even reach out if your pricing isn't posted.

If you make people work hard to try to reach you, many will give up and move on to someone else.

Make It Easy for People to Share about You

If you plan, share and promote your events using social media, this post is specifically for you!

You are so excited about this new idea/annual event/large function you have coming up, right? You love social media and know it's a great place to reach a large audience. Exactly!

Then, let me help you work your event so you can get the most bang for your buck!

- Create a list of "canned" social media posts to share with your champions that they can share with their audiences. This only really works if you do your research! For specific hashtags or keywords, always search first to see how that hashtag might already be in use. (You might be surprised by the results--and not necessarily in a good way.)

- Create a Facebook or LinkedIn event. (or both)

- If you will be hiring a professional photographer, also ask an attendee or two that you know to take pictures that you can post immediately following the event. You are going to spend a great deal of time leading up to the event promoting it, creating buzz, etc. What typically happens with events is there is all sorts of excitement up until that day and then . . . crickets. Your professional photographer could take weeks to get pictures back to you and understandably so, but the people who attended and those who missed out will all be looking for photos right away. If you can get them there to view the photos right away, they will stay engaged longer!

- Ask attendees to share photos and tag you.

Has it seemed to you that Facebook events aren't as effective as they used to be? Here is a short list of do's and don'ts that may help you have more success going forward.

- Don't invite all your friends!

    o I promise you, even if they LOVE you, all your friends won't be able to attend. This would also be the case if you are inviting people from across the country.

    o It makes an event less desirable if you invite 500 people and only five are attending.

- Beware of creating multiple event pages for the same event. This often occurs when there are multiple people helping to plan an event. Each person creates one and then the results get muddied down.

- Don't create an event for things that AREN'T events. (crowdfunding campaigns, weeklong open houses, an invite to like your Facebook business page, etc.)

- Also, don't create a group when what you are really having is an event.

- Invite your guests early enough so they might have an opportunity to come. A lot of invites get posted with only a couple days' notice. Sometimes, that can work to your advantage. Other times, it might flop!

- Create great sharable content about the event. If you make it easy, people are more likely to share.

- Keep the event page active. Treat it similarly to a business page-- post on the event page two to three times per week. When you do that, everyone who RSVPd yes, or hasn't responded will get a notification.

- Ask specific people to share the event or post about it on their Facebook pages, especially your connections with larger networks.

- Post the event in other locations--Eventbrite and Alignable are two great platforms for sharing events.

- Send paper invitations in the mail. This is rarely done anymore, so the impact is greater than what it used to be.

- Pick up the phone and call. Obviously, you can't call everyone, but you could create a list of 10, 15, or 20 people you specifically want to be there!

- Write and distribute a press release when appropriate.

- Send private messages with personal invitations.

Rethink Repurposing

There are so many people, so called "experts" who will share dozens if not 100 ways to repurpose content. The problem with this technique is it keeps you stuck in the hustle. Most of these ideas are around sharing one piece of content to a gazillion different sites.

Sure, there is plenty of time every day to post to multiple platforms, but my guess is, you didn't get into your business to spend all day on social media.

Where does your ideal client hang out or at least the people connected to them? That is where you should invest your efforts.

Make it EASY on yourself!

When I share about repurposing now, I embrace a different idea, which is about using the same content, using it in multiples ways and continuing to use it over and over.

Create Content Once, Use It Forever

Remember earlier when I shared the example of *Vogue* magazine and the idea that they re-create the same thing year after year?

How can you do this in your business? With themes and a content calendar as mentioned before.

Can you take it even further than that?

What if 200 pieces of content could feed your social media forever?

This is a theory I've been testing recently. I created 100+ graphics/memes (made from templates) and a list of questions, quotes and other content bucket ideas I like to talk about on a regular basis.

I started this by hiring a company to go through my Facebook business page and capture every piece of text-only content. What I got back was about 200 "pieces of content" that are evergreen. That content is the same today as it was when I posted it three years ago and will be the same next time I post it as well.

No one will ever notice that you posted the same thing today and six months from now.

This is another way to bring EASE into your marketing.

What are the things you say all the time that can become content you use over and over? What is the advice you share regularly?

With all the noise on social media, if you take this repetitive content and spread it out over the year, chances are you can share the same thing over and over. In fact, sharing the same stories with repetition makes you and those stories more memorable.

I'm not suggesting you just copy and paste and share over and over, but rather take your regular ideas, concepts, and stories and share, adjust, edit, reframe and use again.

YOU MADE IT!

If you have made it this far, congratulations. You deserve to celebrate.

I'm sure you have heard the phrase, "It takes a village to raise a child."

And while you may not need a village, squad or community to grow your business, I promise you that your efforts in creating and building your own will make all the difference in the world.

You aren't in this alone. You were never meant to be. My guess is you have people around you even now who want to support you and cheer you on-- they just may be so involved in building their own empires, they aren't aware.

I didn't write this book to get on any best-seller lists. I wrote it because I really believe--more than ever--that community can change the world.

My hope is that you find yours so you can discover the same.

THANK YOU! I can't wait to hear from you and how the tools in this book are changing the way you do business.

Please feel free to email me at tracey@igniteyourchampions.com, and share your community creation stories!

I look forward to hearing from you and sharing in your success!

REFERENCE

Hashtag Ideas for Visibility

When you create more visibility, you create opportunities for other people to find you and join in your conversations.

Hashtags can be a great strategy for giving your posts more reach on a regular basis.

There are multiple points of view on how many hashtags is too many; it's best to take a "test and see" approach. What hashtags are you using that get engagement? Keep using those!

This isn't about Random Acts of Marketing, but rather forming a systematic and strategic plan that works for you and your business. When you have that, it's easier to hire help in this area.

Bonus note: Please don't share your Instagram posts automatically to Facebook. The language is different because the platform is different, and hashtags tend to not be as effective. Again, this can be a "test and see" to make sure this is true for you.

#MotivationMonday or #MondayMotivation. Start the week on an upbeat note with a motivational picture, video or quote. Bonus if it's branded!

#MondayFunday. Share something fun about you or your business! How do you make your work fun--if that's applicable.

#MusicMonday. People love to know what kind of music you (or your team) favor, and to share theirs. Or you could feature an upcoming concert, or one you attended over the weekend. What songs get you moving every time? It's so fun when you share things like this and you find mutual fan-friends!

#MondayMemories. There are lots of opportunities to share throwbacks. Monday is your first chance of the week! The stories of your business, how you got started and how far you've come are fun ways to invite people into your business. Share old business cards, headshots, pictures of your brick and mortar, etc.

#MindfulMonday or #MantraMonday. Perfect for a business or life coach, yoga studio, and more. Remind your followers and connections to take a deep breath, look at nature, or meditate. Aaah.

#MeowMonday. Um, cats, of course! Not that cat owners need reminders to share their cats, but this gives you/them the perfect excuse. Again, it might seem silly--but animals are another simple way to connect.

#MarketingMonday. Share a tip that's worked for your business. Do you have a campaign that's been really successful? Favorite marketing books or quotes? It's perfect for this day!

#TipTuesday. Perfect for any business! Share your expertise with your followers in a tip or with a graphic. This could be a business tip, productivity tip, money tip, etc.

#TravelTuesday. When it fits, show where your business (or pleasure) has sent you lately.

#TransformationTuesday

#TuesdayTrivia. This is your chance to share statistics about your business or industry. Statistics and trivia can also be great for creating graphics for different platforms.

#TuesdayTraining

#TuesdayTruth

#TuesdayShoesday. Spotlight on fun or interesting shoes in your office!

#TongueOutTuesday or #TOT. Perfect for pets and silly people!

#WellnessWednesday or #HealthyHumpDay or #WednesdayWorkout. If relevant to your business or personal brand, share a health-related tip.

#HumpDay. Celebrate your midweek accomplishments, or the fact that you've made it halfway through the week!

#WisdomWednesday (or #WednesdayWisdom). An opportunity to share a smart business tip.

#WayBackWednesday. Another trip down memory lane!

#WoofWednesday. Dog day! Cats aren't the only pets the internet loves!

#WineWednesday

#ThankfulThursday. Show gratitude to a client, customer, employee, or supporter of your business. Or get your followers thinking positively by asking them to name something they're thankful for.

#TBT or #ThrowbackThursday. The most popular "day of the week" hashtag! Show something you or your company did in years past, your company's growth, or products or services you offered years ago.

#ThursdayThoughts. Share your thoughts on a trending topic in your niche.

#ThinkPositiveThursday. Got a positive thought for Thursday? Share it in a picture quote.

#ThirstyThursday. In the food or health niche? Post a decadent or healthy beverage!

#FF or #FollowFriday or #FeatureFriday. Spotlight another user on the social media platform. They may return the favor later!

#FBF or #FlashbackFriday. When you do throwbacks, the best benefit is you don't have to create new content!

#FridayFunday or #FunnyFriday. Post a meme, or something fun, as people slide into weekend mode.

#FreebieFriday. Do you have a giveaway? Friday is a great day to share it.

#FearlessFriday

#FoodieFriday. Great for food bloggers, restaurants, and fitness businesses, or an awesome opportunity to post a pic of a fabulous meal!

#FeelGoodFriday. Post feel-good photos or quotes that your audience would love.

#Friyay #FridayVibes #FridayFeeling #TGIF. Celebrate that the weekend is here!

#Caturday. Did you miss #MeowMonday? Here's your second chance!

#SaturdaySwag. Perfect to tag products you sell or are giving away in a contest.

#SocialSaturday. Ask your followers a question so you can get to know each other!

#ShoutoutSaturday. Give a shout-out to one of your star employees or best customers.

#SalesSaturday #SaturdaySpecial #SaturdaySale. Offer a Saturday-only discount on your product or services.

#SaturdaySweat. Share your fitness routine or sweaty chores today!

#SmallBusinessSaturday

#SaturdaySweets. Candy stores, bakeries, restaurants, and nutrition experts can share their special treats or a recipe with this tag.

#SS or #SelfieSunday. Where does your Sunday take you?

#SundayFunday. All work and no play is no good! What is something you are doing for fun today?

#SundayRead. Share a recent blog post, or a book you are reading.

#StartupSunday. Share your origin story. What is something that surprised you about starting your company? What is something you wish you had known?

#SpotlightSunday. There are all sorts of things you can spotlight! Get creative!

#SelfcareSunday

Industry-Specific Content Ideas

Content CAN be very simple, but it's also a muscle that needs to be flexed and used on a regular basis.

In the next few pages, you can find some text-only post ideas for specific industries. Please read through them, even if it isn't your business, as you might discover ways you can take these ideas and shift the words to make them work for you.

Event Planners

How many weddings have you attended?

How true do you think the statement, "Always the bridesmaid and never the bride" is?

Does your neighborhood do any community events during the summer?

Have you ever attended a 100th birthday party? Who was the party for?

What is your favorite thing about attending a wedding?

Where did you meet your significant other?

Do you have a photo from a recent photo booth? Please share below.

What song always gets you on the dance floor?

Have you ever been invited to a Quinceañera?

Mortgage Brokers

Did you know, in Scotland, people paint the front door of their house red once they pay off their mortgage?

Do you believe mortgage is boring?

What is something that surprised you when you bought your first home?

Do you know the ten commandments of mortgage?

For you, which came first, mortgage or marriage?

Have you ever thought about buying rental property?

When was the last time you heard from the mortgage broker who helped you with your current home?

Real Estate Agents

What would you rather have in your home, a fireplace, or a soaking bathtub?

Would you rather have a well-landscaped yard, or lots of grass?

Would you rather have a water or mountain view?

Have you ever considered owning rental property?

What does your next home have to have?

When deciding where to live, how important is the walkability score of your new home?

When considering your new neighborhood, how important are the local schools?

Quotes about home

Graphic Designers

How many colors do you use in your branding?

How many fonts do you use in your branding?

What is one word you would use to describe your brand?

Have you ever updated your logo?

When was the last time you updated your branding?

Do you have a branding document you could hand off to someone to get help?

What would you say is the most recognizable logo?

Quotes about creativity

Web Designers

How often do you update your website?

How often do you blog?

Do you love your website?

Does your website bring you qualified leads?

Is your branding consistent between your website, social media, and email templates?

Business and/or Life Coaches

You are the designer and creator of your life. What do those words mean to you?

"A mentor is someone who allows you to see the hope inside yourself." — Oprah Winfrey

Do you believe breakdown comes before the breakthrough?

If you had $5,000 to spend on your business right now, what would you invest in?

Quotes about business, productivity, entrepreneurship, or other coaching specialties.

What is something heard frequently about money when growing up?

What is included in your ideal work week?

Success is scheduled: How do you schedule time to allow for success?

Do you have a mission statement?

What is a mindset block you would like to let go?

What is your top priority for this week?

If I asked you what your goals were, would your calendar reflect your commitment to that goal?

Travel Agents

What is one destination on your bucket list?

What is the favorite place you have taken a cruise?

When you travel, do you like to play it by ear, schedule everything, or something in between?

What is your #1 tip for first time Disney goers?

Have you ever taken a trip by yourself?

Do you travel with your pets?

If money were no object, where would you travel?

Guided or self-guided tours?

Museums/Galleries

Do you have a favorite artist?

Do you consider yourself artistic?

Information about color psychology

What is the most amazing museum you have ever visited?

Do you love black and white photography?

Pet Related Businesses

Do you follow any famous felines on Instagram?

"There is no psychiatrist in the world like a puppy licking your face."
 --Ben Williams

What are your favorite animal rescue organizations?

What is your favorite movie starring a dog or cat?

Who is your favorite cartoon kitty?

Interior Designers

How often do you take time to declutter your home?

Do you love your furniture?

What is one word you would use to describe how you feel about throw pillows?

If you could change one thing about your home, what would that be?

Have you ever lived through a kitchen remodel? What advice would you give to someone going through it right now?

Professional Organizers

Do you have a "junk drawer?"

Would you call yourself organized?

Are you a filer or piler?

Our work is judgement free! What does that mean to you?

General Business Questions

Do you keep a gratitude journal? How has it helped you in your life and business?

How often do you take time to set goals in your business?

How long have you been in your current business?

If you were just starting out, what business advice would you give yourself?

What is the best piece of business advice you have ever received?

What is your favorite business book?

What is a business book you have read more than once?

What is one thing you would like to learn more about to help you in your business?

What is the first thing you outsourced in your business?

How many networking events do you attend in a week/month?

Do you schedule time in your calendar for follow-up?

Emojis in marketing: yay or nay?

Selfie Sunday or Saturday. Ask your audience to share a selfie. (We want to get to know you!)

What is a useful productivity hack you can share with us?

What is a great piece of business advice you've received recently?

If you had an extra $500 (or another amount), what would you invest in? What would you splurge on?

Share a motivational quote that helps you get through tough days.

What is a business tool you cannot live without?

What is an app you use every day?

What is the first app you open on your phone every day?

Is it easy for you to ask for the sale?

What was the last time you did _____?

What is something you would like to learn more about?

What is your business superpower?

How is your week going? Reply with a GIF for added fun. (on Facebook)

What is an accomplishment you are proud of?

You need to get comfortable celebrating your wins. What is one of your victories from this week? Month?

Do you have pets? Share a photo!

Do you need a resource today? How can we help?

What business book are you reading right now?

What podcast are you bingeing?

What is a job you would be terrible at?

What could you give a 30-minute talk about with no preparation?

What's the best thing that has happened to you in the last week?

What website do you visit most often?

What are you excited about in your life or business right now?

What is something you are most proud of?

What is your favorite way to procrastinate?

If a song played when you entered a room, what would it be?

What three words best describe you?

What song always improves your mood?

Are you good at sharing your success?

How much sleep do you need to function well?

What is your favorite thing about owning your own business?

What is the hardest part about owning your own business?

Please share a link to your website.

Have you done business with someone local recently? Please share about them in the comments!

Are you an author? Please share a link to your book.

What is an offer you are making right now that you are excited about?

What is working well in your business right now?

What is important to you outside of business?

What is your greatest strength?

Do you blog? Please share a recent post.

What are your top three core values?

When was the last time you won something?

I would love your ideas for a live video. What would you like to hear me share about?

When was the last time you did something scary?

If you were starting your business over, what advice would you give yourself?

What advice do you wish someone had shared with you when you started your business?

What is an unknown talent you have?

What would you like to be an expert at?

What is one big life goal you have?

What is the best advice you received from your parents?

Have you ever purchased something from an Instagram account or Facebook business page you follow?

Who is your ideal client/customer?

Can you share the link to your Instagram page?

National Holidays

There are holidays for just about everything you can imagine. This can be helpful for creating content, especially if you look ahead to monthly observances, etc. When they relate to your business, it can be a great catalyst for identifying potential themes and content around those themes.

If any of these days have connections to your business and/or expertise, you can use them to create conversations on your social media profiles.

If your champions and advocates have any connections to these days, these can be simple ways to acknowledge them.

Many of these are self-explanatory. When they aren't, I trust you are a skilled search engine user and can find more information. That search might also help you find images for those days unless you want to create something of your own.

January

Hot Tea Month

National Soup Month

National Mentoring Month

Second Wednesday – National Take the Stairs Day

Second Saturday – Vision Board Day

Third Monday – Martin Luther King Jr's Birthday

Last Monday – Bubble Wrap Appreciation Day

Last Saturday – Seed Swap Day

January 1st – Bloody Mary Day

January 2nd – Personal Trainer Awareness Day

January 2nd – National Cream Puff Day

January 3rd – Fruitcake Toss Day

January 3rd – Chocolate Covered Cherry Day

January 4th – National Trivia Day

January 4th – National Spaghetti Day

January 5th – Whipped Cream Day

January 8th – National Bubble Bath Day

January 9th – National Law Enforcement Appreciation Day

January 10th – Save the Eagles Day

January 10th – Houseplant Appreciation Day

January 12th – Kiss a Ginger Day (with consent, of course)

January 12th – National Pharmacist Day

January 12th – National Hot Tea Day

January 13th – National Sticker Day

January 13th – Make Your Dreams Come True Day

January 13th – National Rubber Ducky Day

January 14th – Clean off Your Desk Day

January 14th – National Dress up Your Pet Day

January 15th – Strawberry Ice Cream Day

January 15th – National Bagel Day

January 15th – National Hat Day

January 16th – Appreciate a Dragon Day (*Game of Thrones* fans?)

January 18th – Winnie the Pooh Day

January 18th – Thesaurus Day

January 19th – National Popcorn Day

January 20th – National DJ Day

January 20th – Penguin Awareness Day

January 20th – National Cheese Lovers Day

January 21st – National Hugging Day

January 24th – National Compliment Day

January 25th – Opposite Day

January 27th – National Chocolate Cake Day

January 28th – Community Manager Appreciation Day
(Thank your social media manager!)

January 28th – Have Fun at Work Day

January 29th – Puzzle Day

January 31st – Inspire Your Heart with Art Day

January 31st – National Backward Day

February

National Cherry Month

American Heart Month

Black History Month

National Bird Feeding Month

First Friday – Bubble Gum Day

First Saturday – Eat Ice Cream for Breakfast Day

February 2nd – National Tater Tot Day

February 3rd – National Carrot Cake Day

February 3rd – Women Physicians Day

February 3rd – Feed the Birds Day

February 4th – National Thank a Mail Carrier Day

February 4th – National Homemade Soup Day

February 5th – World Nutella Day

February 5th – National Weather Person's Day

February 5th – International Girls and Women in Sports Day

February 6th – Dentists Day

February 6th – National Frozen Yogurt Day

February 7th – Send a Card to a Friend Day

February 8th – National Boy Scouts Day

February 9th – National Pizza Day

February 10th – Umbrella Day

February 11th – National Inventors Day

February 11th – Clean Out Your Computer Day

February 11th – National Make a Friend Day

February 14th – National Organ Donor Day

February 16th – National Do a Grouch a Favor Day
　　　　　　　(You might not want to share what you are celebrating.)

February 17th – Random Acts of Kindness Day

February 18th – National Drink Wine Day

February 19th – National Chocolate Mint Day

February 20th – Love Your Pet Day (Isn't that every day?)

February 22nd – National Margarita Day

February 23rd – Tennis Day

February 24th – National Tortilla Chip Day

February 25th – National Clam Chowder Day

February 26th – Tell a Fairy Tale Day

February 26th – National Pistachio Day

February 27th – National Strawberry Day

February 27th – Polar Bear Day

February 28th – Floral Design Day

March

National Craft Month

National Peanut Month

Women's History Month

Youth Art Month

National Colon Cancer Awareness Month

Red Cross Month

First Friday – Employee Appreciation Day

First Friday – World Prayer Day

Second Saturday – Genealogy Day

Third Saturday – National Quilting Day

March 1st – Peanut Butter Lovers Day

March 1st – World Compliment Day

March 2nd – Dr. Seuss Day (his birthday)

March 2nd – National Banana Cream Pie Day

March 3rd – National Soup It Forward Day

March 3rd – Peach Blossom Day

March 4th – National Grammar Day

March 5th – National Pancake Day

March 6th – National Oreo Cookie Day

March 6th – National Frozen Food Day

March 8th – National Proofreading Day

March 8th – International Women's Day

March 9th – National Napping Day

March 9th – Picnic Day

March 10th – International Day of Awesomeness

March 10th – Middle Name Pride Day

March 11th – Napping Day

March 12th – Girls Scouts Day

March 12th – Plant a Flower Day

March 14th – Popcorn Lovers Day

March 14th – National Potato Chip Day

March 14th – Pi Day

March 19th – National Chocolate Caramel Day

March 19th – National Let's Laugh Day

March 20th – International Day of Happiness

March 20th – International Earth Day

March 21st – National French Bread Day

March 22nd – National Goof Off Day

March 23rd – National Chip and Dip Day

March 23rd – National Puppy Day

March 24th – National Chocolate Covered Raisins Day

March 25th – Pecan Day

March 25th – Waffle Day

March 28th – National Something on a Stick Day
       (What is your favorite food that is served on a stick?)

March 29th – National Mom and Pop Business Owners Day

March 31st – National Crayon Day

April

Stress Awareness Month (Is there anyone NOT aware of stress?)

Autism Awareness Month

Financial Literacy Month

Jazz Appreciation Month

National Volunteer Month

National Child Abuse Prevention Month

National Poetry Month

Sexual Assault Awareness Month

First Friday – Walk to Work Day

Third Thursday – High Fives Day

Fourth Thursday – Take Your Daughter to Work Day

Last Friday – Arbor Day

April 1st – April Fools' Day

April 1st – International Fun at Work Day

April 1st – Sourdough Bread Day

April 2nd – Equal Pay Day

April 2nd – Children's Book Day

April 2nd – National Peanut Butter and Jelly Day

April 3rd – National Walking Day

April 5th – Deep Dish Pizza Day

April 6th – Caramel Popcorn Day

April 7th – No Housework Day

April 7th – National Beer Day

April 9th – Be Kind to Lawyers Day

April 10th – Golf Day

April 11th – National Pet Day

April 11th – Barbershop Quartet Day

April 12th – Grilled Cheese Sandwich Day

April 12th – National Licorice Day

April 13th – Scrabble Day

April 16th – National Wear Your Pajamas to Work Day

April 17th – International Haiku Poetry Day
      (Can you create a Haiku for your business?)

April 18th – National High-Five Day

April 19th – National Garlic Day

April 20th – Volunteer Recognition Day

April 22nd – Girl Scout Leader's Day

April 22nd – Administrative Professionals Day

April 22nd – Jellybean Day (What's your favorite jellybean flavor?)

April 23rd – Talk Like Shakespeare Day

April 25th – Hug a Plumber Day

April 25th – World Penguin Day

April 26th – National Pretzel Day

April 29th – International Dance Day

April 30th – Adopt a Shelter Pet Day

April 30th – Oatmeal Cookie Day

April 30th – Bugs Bunny Day

May

National Barbecue Month

National Salad Month

ALS Awareness Month

Asian Pacific American Heritage Month

Celiac Awareness Month

Mental Health Awareness Month

National Foster Care Month

National Pet Month

National Stroke Awareness Month

Tuesday of the first full week – Teacher Appreciation Day

Friday before Mother's Day – Military Spouse Appreciation Day

Second Sunday – Mother's Day

Third Friday – National Bike to Work Day

Third Saturday – Armed Forces Day

May 1st – Mother Goose Day

May 2nd – World Password Day

May 2nd – National Life Insurance Day

May 3rd – No Pants Day

May 4th – Star Wars Day

May 4th – International Firefighters Day

May 6th – Nurses Day

May 6th – No Diet Day

May 7th – Thank a Teacher Day

May 8th – No Socks Day

May 9th – National Moscato Day

May 10th – Clean Up Your Room Day

May 11th – Eat What You Want Day

May 11th – Twilight Zone Day

May 12th – International Nurses Day

May 13th – National Apple Pie Day

May 14th – National Dance Like a Chicken Day

May 15th – National Chocolate Chip Day

May 15th – Endangered Species Day

May 16th – Do Something Good for Your Neighbor Day

May 16th – National Love a Tree Day

May 17th – Pizza Party Day

May 18th – International Museum Day

May 18th – Visit Your Relatives Day

May 18th – No Dirty Dishes Day
   (Sounds like a great excuse to buy paper plates!)

May 20th – National Rescue Dog Day

May 21st – National Waitstaff Day

May 21st – Talk Like Yoda Day

May 24th – National Scavenger Hunt Day (Could be a great day to plan a digital scavenger hunt for your business.)

May 25th – National Wine Day

May 28th – National Hamburger Day

May 30th – National Creativity Day

May 31st – Macaroon Day

June

African-American Music Appreciation Month

Alzheimer's and Brain Awareness Month

LGBT Pride Month

Candy Month

Dairy Month

Turkey Lovers Month

First Friday – Donut Day

First Sunday – National Frozen Yogurt Day

First Sunday – National Cancer Survivor's Day

Friday after Father's Day – Take your Dog to Work Day

June 1st – National Say Something Nice Day

June 2nd – National Rocky Road Day

June 2nd – Leave the Office Early Day

June 4th – National Cheese Day

June 4th – Hug Your Cat Day

June 6th – Drive in Movie Day

June 7th – Chocolate Ice Cream Day

June 9th – Donald Duck Day

June 10th – National Iced Tea Day

June 11th – Corn on the Cob Day

June 12th – National Peanut Butter Cookie Day

June 14th – World Blood Donor Day

June 14th – International Bath Day

June 17th – National Eat Your Vegetables Day

June 18th – International Picnic Day

June 19th – National Martini Day

June 19th – National Kissing Day

June 19th – National Garfield the Cat Day
    (Could be the perfect opportunity to have lasagna!)

June 20th – Ice Cream Soda Day

June 21st – National Selfie Day (Isn't that every day?)

June 21st – International Yoga Day

June 22nd – Chocolate Éclair Day

June 30th – Social Media Day

July

National Ice Cream Month

Third Wednesday – National Hot Dog Day

Third Sunday – National Ice Cream Day

Last Friday – System Administrator Appreciation Day

July 1st – International Joke Day
               (To pun, or not to pun. Is that the question?)

July 1st – Postal Worker Day

July 1st – US Postage Stamp Day

July 2nd – World UFO Day

July 4th – National Caesar Salad Day

July 6th – National Fried Chicken Day

July 7th – World Chocolate Day

July 7th – World Macaroni Day

July 9th – National Sugar Cookie Day

July 10th – National Pina Colada Day

July 10th – Teddy Bear Picnic Day

July 11th – National Blueberry Muffin Day

July 11th – Mojito Day

July 13th – National French Fry Day

July 13th – National Barbershop Music Appreciation Day

July 14th – Mac & Cheese Day

July 17th – National Tattoo Day

July 17th – World Emoji Day (Comment with your most used/
               favorite emoji)

July 18th – Get to Know Your Customers Day

July 20th – Lollipop Day

July 21st – National Junk Food Day

July 23rd – Hot Dog Day

July 25th – Hot Fudge Sundae Day

July 26th – Bert (from Sesame Street) Birthday

July 27th – National Dance Day

July 28th – Milk Chocolate Day

July 29th – National Lipstick Day

July 29th – National Lasagna Day

July 30th – Cheesecake Day

July 31st – National Mutt Day

August

Family Fun Month

First Sunday – National Friendship Day

First Sunday – Sisters Day

Second Saturday – Garage Sale Day

Third Saturday – Honeybee Awareness Day

August 2nd – National Coloring Book Day

August 2nd – National Ice Cream Sandwich Day

August 2nd – International Beer Day

August 3rd – National Watermelon Day

August 4th – Chocolate Chip Cookie Day

August 6th – Fresh Breath Day

August 6th – Root Beer Float Day

August 8th – International Cat Day

August 8th – Sneak Some Zucchini onto Your Neighbor's Porch Day
(If you've ever grow zucchini, you understand!)

August 8th – Happiness Happens Day

August 9th – National Booklovers Day

August 10th – National Lazy Day

August 10th – National S'mores Day

August 11th – National Presidential Joke Day

August 13th – International Lefthanders Day

August 14th – National Creamsicle Day

August 15th – National Relaxation Day

August 16th – National Tell a Joke Day

August 17th – National Thrift Shop Day

August 17th – Black Cat Appreciation Day

August 19th – National Potato Day

August 20th – National Lemonade Day

August 22nd – Be an Angel Day

August 22nd – Tooth Fairy Day

August 24th – National Waffle Day

August 25th – Banana Split Day

August 26th – National Dog Day

August 26th – Women's Equality Day

August 27th - Global Forgiveness Day

August 30th – Toasted Marshmallow Day

August 31st – National Trail Mix Day

September

Gospel Music Heritage Month

National Hispanic Heritage Month

National Honey Month

National Preparedness Month

National Yoga Month

Pain Awareness Month

Self-Improvement Month

Saturday before Labor Day – International Bacon Day

September 5th – Cheese Pizza Day

September 6th – Read a Book Day

September 7th – National Salami Day

September 8th – Oncology Nurses Day

September 9th – National Teddy Bear Day

September 10th – World Suicide Prevention Day

September 10th – Grandparents Day

September 12th – National Day of Encouragement

September 12th – Chocolate Milkshake Day

September 13th – Stand Up to Cancer Day

September 13th – Positive Thinking Day

September 13th – Fortune Cookie Day

September 14th – Cream Filled Donut Day

September 16th – Mexican Independence Day

September 16th – National Play Doh Day

September 17th – National IT Professionals Day

September 18th – National Cheeseburger Day

September 19th – Talk Like a Pirate Day

September 19th – Butterscotch Pudding Day

September 19th – National Gymnastics Day

September 20th – National Pepperoni Pizza Day

September 21st – Mini Golf Day

September 21st – World Gratitude Day

September 22nd – Car Free Day

September 22nd – Businesswomen's Day

September 23rd – National Great American Pot Pie Day

September 24th – National Punctuation Day

September 25th – National One Hit Wonder Day (What is YOUR favorite?)

September 25th – Comic Book Day (Marvel or DC?)

September 28th – National Family Health and Fitness Day

September 28th – National Good Neighbor Day

September 29th – International Coffee Day

September 30th – International Podcast Day

September 30th – National Chewing Gum Day

October

Breast Cancer Awareness Month

Filipino American History Month

Italian American Heritage and Culture Month

LGBT History Month

National Arts & Humanities Month

National Bullying Prevention Month

National Cyber Security Awareness Month

National Hispanic Heritage Month (September 15 – October 15)

National Pizza Month

National Domestic Violence Awareness Month

First Saturday – International Frugal Fun Day

First Saturday – World Card Making Day

Second Monday – Indigenous People's Day

Second Wednesday – Take Your Teddy Bear to Work Day

Second Wednesday – Stop Bullying Day

Third Monday – Clean Your Virtual Desktop Day

Third Wednesday – Support Your Local Chamber of Commerce Day

Third Friday – National Mammography Day

Fourth Saturday – Make a Difference Day

October 1st – World Vegetarian Day

October 1st – National Homemade Cookies Day

October 2nd – Name Your Car Day (Does your car have a name?)

October 2nd – National Custodian Day

October 3rd – Techies Day

October 4th – National Taco Day

October 4th – World Smile Day

October 4th – National Golf Day

October 5th – World Teachers' Day

October 5th – National Do Something Nice Day

October 10th – World Mental Health Day

October 10th – National Hug a Drummer Day

October 11th – National Coming Out Day

October 14th – National Dessert Day

October 15th – National Grouch Day

October 16th – World Food Day

October 16th – Bosses Day

October 16th – Dictionary Day

October 17th – National Pasta Day

October 18th – National Chocolate Cupcake Day

October 20th – World Statistics Day

October 20th – International Chef's Day

October 23rd – National Boston Cream Pie Day

October 25th – Greasy Foods Day

October 25th – World Pasta Day

October 26th - National Pumpkin Pie Day

October 26th – National Make a Difference Day

October 27th – National Mentoring Day

October 28th – National Chocolate Day

October 28th – National First Responders Day

October 29th – National Cat Day

October 30th – Checklist Day

October 30th – National Candy Corn Day (Yay or nay?)

October 31st – National Magic Day

October 31st – Knock-Knock Jokes Day

November

Movember - November events to raise awareness and funds for men's health issues, such as prostate cancer and depression

National Family Caregivers Month

National Novel Writing Month – Also called NaNoWriMo

Native American Indian/Alaska Native Heritage Month

Saturday before Thanksgiving – National Adoption Day

Day After Thanksgiving – Buy Nothing Day

Saturday After Thanksgiving – Small Business Saturday

November 1st – World Vegan Day

November 1st – National Authors Day

November 2nd – Deviled Egg Day

November 3rd – National Sandwich Day

November 4th – National Candy Day

November 4th – Use Your Common Sense Day

November 6th – Stress Awareness Day

November 6th – National Nachos Day

November 8th – STEM Day

November 10th – National Vanilla Cupcake Day

November 10th – International Accounting Day

November 11th – National Sundae Day

November 12th – Chicken Soup for the Soul Day

November 13th – World Kindness Day

November 14th – National Pickle Day

November 15th – America Recycles Day

November 15th – Clean Out Your Refrigerator Day

November 16th – National Fast Food Day

November 17th – National Take a Hike Day

November 18th – National Princess Day

November 18th – Mickey Mouse's Birthday

November 19th – National Entrepreneurs Day

November 19th – National Play Monopoly Day

November 23rd – National Cashew Day

November 23rd – National Espresso Day

November 28th – National French Toast Day

November 30th – Computer Security Day

December

December 1st – Eat a Red Apple Day

December 2nd – National Special Education Day

December 4th – National Sock Day

December 5th – International Ninja Day

December 5th – Bathtub Party Day

December 7th – Cotton Candy Day

December 7th – Letter Writing Day

December 8th – Brownie Day

December 8th – National Bartender Day

December 12th – National Poinsettia Day

December 13th – National Salesperson Day

December 16th – National Chocolate Covered Everything Day

December 18th – Answer the Phone Like Buddy the Elf Day
> "(Insert Your Name) the Elf, what's your favorite color?"

December 21st – Crossword Puzzle Day

December 23rd – Festivus

December 28th – Card Playing Day

December 31st – Champagne Day

Sources

HolidayInsights.com

NationalDayCalendar.com

HolidaysCalendar.com

Timeanddate.com

https://en.wikipedia.org/wiki/List_of_month-long_observances

Books Referenced

Radha Agrawal, *Belong: Find Your People, Create Community, and Live a More Connected Life* (New York: Workman Publishing Company, 2018)

Brene Brown, *Dare to Lead: Brave Work. Tough Conversations. Whole Hearts.* (New York: Random House, 2018)

Glennon Doyle, *Untamed* (New York: The Dial Press, 2020)

Nancy McSharry Jensen and Sarah Duenwald, *Back to Business: Finding Your Confidence, Embracing Your Skills, and Landing Your Dream Job After a Career Pause* (New York: Harper Collins, 2021)

Michelle A. Mazur, Ph.D., *3 Word Rebellion: Create a One-of-a-Kind Message that Grows Your Business into a Movement* (Seattle: Communication Rebel Press, 2019)

Simon Sinek, *Start with Why* (TED Talk, 2009)

Bernadette Jiwa, *Story Driven: You Don't Need to Compete when You Know Who You Are* (Australia: Perceptive Press, 2018)

Nilofer Merchant, *The Power of Onlyness: Make Your Wild Ideas Mighty Enough to Dent the World* (New York: Viking, 2017)

David Meerman Scott, Reiko Scott, *Fanocracy: Turning Fans into Customers and Customers into Fans* (New York: Portfolio/Penguin, 2020)

Tim S. Grover, *Shari Lesser Wenk, Relentless: From Good to Great to Unstoppable* (New York: Scribner, 2013)

Shawn Achor, *Big Potential: How Transforming the Pursuit of Success Raises Our Achievement, Happiness, and Well-Being* (New York: Currency, 2018)

Matthew Kelly, *The Rhythm of Life: Living Every Day with Passion & Purpose* (Blue Sparrow, 2015)

Denise Duffield-Thomas, *Chillpreneur: The New Rules for Creating Success, Freedom, and Abundance on Your Terms* (Carlsbad, CA: Hayhouse Inc., 2020)

Dave Kerpen, *The Art of People: 11 Simple People Skills That Will Get You Everything You Want* (New York: Penguin, 2017)

Bri Seeley, *Permission to Leap: The Six-Phase Journey to Bring Your Vision to Life* (Seeley Enterprises, Inc., 2017)

Nikki Rausch, *Six-Word Lessons on Influencing with Grace: 100 Lessons to Genuinely Connect with Colleagues, Friends, Family and Lovers* (Bellevue WA: Pacelli Publishing, 2017)

Nikki Rausch, *Buying Signals: Turn Casual Conversations into Sales* (Bellevue, WA: Pacelli Publishing, 2016)

Nikki Rausch, *The Selling Staircase: Mastering the Art of Relationship Selling* (Independently Published, 2019)

Individuals Quoted

Michelle L. Evans, Accelaris

Kelly Smith, Willow and Oak Solutions

Nikki Rausch, Sales Maven

Sally Hogshead, CEO of Fascinate Inc.

Amy Porterfield, host of *Marketing Made Easy* podcast

Made in the USA
Columbia, SC
12 September 2021